Narrative Theology in
Early Jewish Christianity

Narrative Theology in Early Jewish Christianity

William Richard Stegner

WJKP

Westminster / John Knox Press
Louisville, Kentucky

Library of Congress Cataloging-in-Publication Data

Stegner, William Richard. 1930–
    Narrative theology in early Jewish Christianity / William Richard
Stegner.
      p. cm.
    Bibliography: p.
    Includes index.
    ISBN 0-8042-0265-6
    1. Bible. N.T. Gospels—Criticism, interpretation, etc.
2. Narration in the Bible. 3. Jewish Christians—History—Early
church, ca. 30–600. I. Title.
BS2555.2.S724   1989
226'.06—dc19   89-5251
                                                   CIP

10 9 8 7 6 5 4 3 2 1
Printed in the United States of America
Westminster/John Knox Press
Louisville, Kentucky

Acknowledgments

Unless otherwise indicated, Scripture quotations are from the Revised Standard Version of the Holy Bible, copyright, 1946, 1952, and © 1971, 1973 by the Division of Christian Education, National Council of the Churches of Christ in the U.S.A., and used by permission.

Acknowledgment is made for permission to reprint from the following sources:

To E. J. Brill for excerpts from Wayne Meeks, *The Prophet-King: Moses Traditions and the Johannine Christology,* copyright 1967 by E. J. Brill, and from Geza Vermes, *Scripture and Tradition in Judaism,* copyright 1973 by E. J. Brill.

To Doubleday for excerpt from THE OLD TESTAMENT PSEUDEPIGRAPHA Vols. I and II edited by James H. Charlesworth. Copyright © 1983 and 1985 by James H. Charlesworth. Reprinted by permission of Doubleday, a division of Bantam, Doubleday, Dell Publishing Group, Inc. For excerpt from THE GOSPEL ACCORDING TO LUKE I–IX (Anchor Bible) edited and translated by Joseph A. Fitzmyer. Copyright © 1981 by Doubleday, a division of Bantam, Doubleday, Dell Publishing Group, Inc. Reprinted by permission of the publisher.

To Bertil Gärtner for excerpts from his *John 6 and the Jewish Passover,* Coniectanea Neotestamentica XVII, copyright © 1959 by Bertil E. Gärtner and used by permission.

To Harvard University Press for excerpt from F. Josephus, *Jewish Antiquities,* volume 4, translated by H. St. J. Thackeray, copyright 1957 by Harvard University Press.

To Irish Academic Press for excerpt from Martin McNamara, *Targum and Testament: Aramaic Paraphrases of the Hebrew Bible: A Light on the New Testament,* copyright by Irish Academic Press and used by permission.

To Judson Press for excerpts from Howard Kee, "The Transfiguration in Mark" in *Understanding the Sacred Text,* edited by John Reumann, copyright 1972 by Judson Press and used by permission of Judson Press.

To Howard Clark Kee for excerpts from his *Community of the New Age: Studies in Mark's Gospel,* copyright 1982 by Howard Clark Kee.

To Macmillan Publishing Company for excerpt reprinted by permission of Charles Scribner's Sons, an imprint of Macmillan Publishing Company from FROM TRADITION TO GOSPEL by Martin Dibelius. (New York 1935)

To The Westminster Press for excerpts reprinted from THE RULE OF QUMRAN AND ITS MEANING, by A.R.C. Leaney. © SCM Press Ltd., 1966. Published in the U.S.A. by The Westminster Press. Reprinted and used by permission.

To the *Journal of Biblical Literature* for excerpt from Harry L. Chronis, "The Torn Veil: Cultus and Christology in Mark 15:37–39," *Journal of Biblical Literature* 101 (1982).

To the *Journal of Jewish Studies* for excerpt from Robert Hayward, "The Present State of Research into the Targumic Account of the Sacrifice of Isaac," *Journal of Jewish Studies* 32 (Autumn 1981).

Appreciation

Since this book was written over a period of several years, my debt of gratitude to persons and institutions is great. I am especially grateful to the administration and trustees of Garrett-Evangelical Theological Seminary for the sabbatical year during which most of the book was written, to the Association of Theological Schools for a generous grant that made study at Oxford possible, to the Oxford Centre for Postgraduate Hebrew Studies, which furnished housing at Yarnton, to Dr. Geza Vermes who generously read and criticized the chapters as I wrote them, to Dr. Eugene Mihaly who opened to me the world of midrash, to Helen Hauldren, our diligent faculty secretary, who typed and proofread the manuscript, and to my wife, Elizabeth, whose encouragement and support were constantly available. To these and others I express my heartfelt thanks.

Contents

Introduction   1

The Words of the Title   2
The Significance of Story   3
Methodological Questions   5

**1. The Baptism of Jesus
and the Binding of Isaac**   13

A Method of Approach   14
The Main Thrust of the Story   15
Words from Genesis 22   17
The Jewish Tradition: Form Criticism   20
The Jewish Tradition in the Targums   22
The Work of Early Jewish Christians   24
The Theological Significance of the Two Scenes   26
Dating the Targumic Material   28
Conclusions   30

2. The Temptation of Jesus   33

Critical Issues   33
Words from the Greek Bible   36
The Jewish Tradition: The Dead Sea Scrolls   37
The Jewish Exegetical Tradition   40
The Didactic Activity of Early Jewish Christians   45
Conclusions   48

3. The Feeding of the Five Thousand 53

Critical Issues 53
Words from the Greek Bible 61
The Jewish Tradition 72
The Work of Early Jewish Christians 74
The Theological Significance of the Story 77

4. The Transfiguration 83

Critical Issues 83
Details and Words from the Greek Bible 87
The Jewish Tradition 91
The Work of Early Jewish Christians 95
The Theological Significance of the Story 99

5. Conclusion 105

Unique Aspects of the Foregoing Study 105
The Exodus/Sinai/Wilderness Motif 107
Christology 110
The Self-understanding of Early Jewish Christians 111
Beyond the Evidence 114
Further Implications 116

Notes 119

Index of Subjects and Names 131

Index of References 139

Introduction

Authors have used the words *Jewish Christianity* in a variety of ways. In a number of studies, for example, this phrase describes the Ebionites who flourished in the second and third centuries A.D. Consequently, I have added the word *early* to designate a first-century community which existed between the resurrection of Jesus and the destruction of Jerusalem in A.D. 70.

Who were these Jewish Christians? Since Jesus was a Jew and nearly all his early followers were Jewish, the words *Jewish Christianity* could describe most members of the earliest church. According to the New Testament, the first or earliest church began in Jerusalem, and the book of Acts indicates that Jerusalem was the church's headquarters; thus Jerusalem was not the only Jewish Christian church. In his first letter to the Thessalonians, Paul refers to "the churches of God in Christ Jesus which are in Judaea" (2:14). Apparently the church in Damascus where Paul was converted was also Jewish Christian. Other Jewish Christian groups may have existed in Galilee and nearby cities, but we have no evidence of them.

The Jerusalem congregation continued until the outbreak of the Jewish-Roman war (A.D. 66–70). According to tradition, the congregation left Jerusalem before it was besieged and conquered by the Romans, and fled to the city of Pella, located on the other side of the Jordan River in what is now the modern kingdom of Jordan. After the flight to Pella, Jewish Christianity seems to have split into a number of branches or sects, one of which was called the Ebionites. Whether the Ebionites were an offshoot of the Jerusalem church (now located in Pella) or just a parallel group of Jewish Christians is not clear. The

Ebionites are mentioned by two of the church fathers, and several of their written works have survived.

From the church fathers' accounts and from the Ebionites' own works, we can reconstruct several distinguishing marks of Ebionite thought and theology. The sect faithfully observed circumcision, the sabbath, and other provisions of the Jewish law. They looked upon the Apostle Paul as their great enemy, believing that he did not truly represent the teachings of Jesus. Also, they considered Jesus the greatest of the prophets, a man whose mission was primarily that of teaching.[1]

The Words of the Title

Nearly every word in the title of this book needs clarification. Although Jewish Christians continued to exist after the destruction of Jerusalem in A.D. 70, this study covers only the early period before that date—the time during which the main literary sources of this study appeared. Thus the time span of the stories analyzed in this book, and their theological motifs, establish a *fixed point of reference* for the study of early Jewish Christianity. Previous inquiries into Jewish Christianity, largely studies of the Ebionites, unfortunately rely upon later sources which are hard to date, since they have been edited and interpolated in the process of transmission. In contrast, the data for this book comes from the New Testament and is datable several years before A.D. 70.

The term *Jewish*, when prefixed to the word *Christianity*, also needs explanation. In order to define the phrase with precision, I follow Richard Longenecker, who uses it "ideologically." Thus the phrase *Jewish Christians* indicates "early Christians whose conceptual frame of reference and whose expressions were rooted in Semitic thought generally and Judaism in particular."[2] Consequently these early Jewish Christians expressed their new faith in Jesus in a way compatible with their Jewish background. Each of the succeeding chapters depicts this understanding of Jesus.

The word *theology*, too, may raise some questions. This book does not claim to be *the* theology of early Jewish Christianity. It is not a complete theology; it makes no attempt to cover the topics traditionally discussed in a theology textbook. In addition, in discussing the significance of Jesus for Jewish Christianity I do not aim at any precise definition of such familiar titles as "Messiah" or "Son of Man." Rather, I merely focus on several stories or narratives dating from the early Jewish Christian period. While other means of expression were open to these people, the Jewish Christians who formulated these stories chose the medium of narrative to portray their faith in Jesus. I simply claim that these stories do represent the theological reflections of Jewish Christians between the death of Jesus and the destruction of Jerusalem.

Finally, I use the term *narrative* to emphasize that Jewish Christians sometimes depicted their theology through stories. Narrative, therefore, is here distinct from the new approach to biblical study called "narrative criticism." This school of criticism, as it is applied to the New Testament, seeks to examine a whole Gospel, such as Mark, as a continuous story—including such categories as plot, character development, conflict, and so forth. Such an approach does not work well with the individual stories that are the literary deposits of Jewish Christianity.

The closest this book comes to narrative criticism is its examination of the temptation narrative in chapter 2. There the conflict takes place between the protagonist Jesus as the Son of God and his opponent, the devil. This conflict brings out the distinguishing character trait of Jesus: his obedience to God. In addition, the words that Jesus quotes from the Hebrew Bible explain the meaning of his temptations. While narrative criticism is helpful in analyzing an entire Gospel, it adds little to the analysis of the other three narratives discussed in this book.

The Significance of Story

Some Jewish Christians communicated their theological reflections in story, just as Jesus taught religious truth through parables. Such narrative communication, however, does not occupy a prominent place in contemporary education. Thus first-century Jewish modes of thought contrast strongly with teaching methods today. Modern higher education relies heavily upon lectures, which supposedly present clear statements and well-organized units of thought. Listeners expect topics to be developed by main points, subsidiary points, and so on. Consequently the Jewish Christians' transmission of religious thought through narrative poses two immediate difficulties for the modern interpreter. The first of these is our temptation simply to state the meaning of the story in sentences. Then, of course, the story is no longer necessary. As in the case of parables, however, the "meaning" cannot live apart from the story because the story always conveys far more than what the reader can reduce to flat propositional statements. Rather, the interpreter must learn to work *through* the story and state the meaning *in terms of the story*. This is no easy task, because it means entering into the world of the story.

'I'he second difficulty is the fact that Jewish Christians lived out of the Hebrew Bible in a way most moderns do not understand. Questions of religion, law, education, and agriculture, and also private matters such as diet, clothing, sexual practice, and daily scheduling, were all biblically centered. Consequently it should not surprise us that early Jewish Christians borrowed from Old Testament stories to express their faith in Jesus. The narrative of Jesus' temptation, for example, contains integral ties to three stories about Israel's experience in the Sinai wilderness. In the first story the children of Israel, newly led out of Egyptian bondage, grumble because there is no food in the wilderness; God responds by giving them manna to eat (Exod. 16). Shortly thereafter, "there was no water for the people to drink" (Exod. 17:1), and so at Massah they put God to the test by demanding water as proof of God's support and presence. The third story is more difficult to pinpoint. Several times during the wilderness wanderings the children of Israel pursued other gods, although the worship of the golden calf (Exod. 32) is the most familiar. Jewish commentators later fastened on this incident as the Hebrews' most serious sin.

The method by which Jewish Christians related Jesus to stories from the Hebrew Bible is called typology, an ancient method of biblical interpretation in which Old Testament persons, events, or things represent "types" or foreshadowings of similar persons, events, and things in the New Testament (hereafter referred to as NT). For example, in 1 Corinthians 10:2–4, Paul interprets Israel's passing through the Red Sea as a "type" or foreshadowing of Christian baptism. Similarly, the manna and the water in the wilderness fore-shadow the bread and wine of the Lord's Supper.

Typology seeks to relate two historical persons or events because it presupposes that God acts in history. God's actions through a person or event in one era predict the way God will act in a subsequent age. Moreover Saint Paul and other NT writers believed that God's act in the life of Jesus was the climax and fulfillment of all God's saving activity in past times. In this way typology resembles some symphonic music: a theme or melody which occurs at the beginning of a work is repeated later on a higher and grander level. The first deliverance from Egyptian bondage thus foreshadows the final, grander deliv-erance from sin and death in Jesus' crucifixion and resurrection.

Because of the difficulties involved in entering into the world of the stories formulated by these Jewish Christians, questions of method-ology almost inevitably arise.

Methodological Questions

The modern interpreter of these early Jewish Christian stories must consider at least two methodological questions. The first involves the proper method for entering into the world of the story, and the second concerns the dating of certain Jewish traditions which the stories presuppose.

Before critics can explore a work's meaning, they must know some-thing about the "form" of that piece of literature. Is it prose or poetry? Is it fact or fiction? Certainly, a critic does not arrive at the meaning of a poem or novel in the same way one arrives at the meaning of a scientific report or textbook. New Testament interpreters, too, are concerned with form. In NT research, scholars called "form critics" have tried to classify the kinds of stories found in the Gospels. For example, miracle stories follow a particular pattern or form, usually consisting of three parts: the setting, which describes the circum-stances of the miracle; the description of the wonder itself, such as a healing; and then the awe-filled response of the audience. A parable, by contrast, usually has only two parts. It describes some everyday happening or phenomenon of nature, such as the life cycle of a mustard plant, and compares it to God's dealing with humans.

However, in their attempts to classify the narratives of early Jewish Christians, form critics have failed to arrive at any consensus. They suggest widely different conclusions about the form and thus also about the meaning of each story. The story of the feeding of the five thousand illustrates such a controversy. One critic classifies this story as a nature miracle, thereby emphasizing the wonder itself; accordingly the story means primarily that hungry people were miraculously fed. More recent critics call the story an epiphany, in that the miracle points beyond itself to the significance of the miracle worker. Since an epiphany deals with the appearance of the divine on earth, the story's meaning is thus the godlike quality of Jesus' activity. Another critic labels the story a symbolic miracle, whose meaning points beyond that miracle, again, to someone or something else. Yet no specific directions are given for arriving at the symbolic dimension of the story. Form criticism, although it has successfully categorized other Gospel narratives, has not provided adequate classification of these early Jewish Christian stories. We must therefore look to another method for exploring the meaning of these narratives.

Birger Gerhardsson has proposed a method of analysis that may fill in the gap left by form critics. He describes his approach as "a method of genetic analysis of one particular type of gospel tradition"[3]—that is, of stories such as the temptation narrative, which can be traced to Jewish Christianity. "Genetic analysis" means an examination in terms of three specific constituent elements. Unlike some form critics, Gerhardsson is not trying to make abstract "forms" fit specific stories; rather, he is examining elements found within the stories themselves. The following paragraphs apply Gerhardsson's method to the narrative of Jesus' wilderness temptation, as found in Matthew's Gospel.

The first of Gerhardsson's constituent elements consists of words from the Hebrew Bible, usually the Torah. In this story the words come from Deuteronomy 8:3 and Deuteronomy 6:16 and 13, which allude to the Israelites' sojourn in the wilderness. According to each story, Israel did not trust God. The hungry people grumbled, became frightened, tested God, and finally turned to another deity. Note the increasing gravity of their disobedience!

The second constituent element is a broad category best described as Jewish tradition, here consisting mostly of exegetical traditions which interpreted the word *wilderness*. Exegetical traditions are customary ways of interpreting words and passages of Scripture, and they enable the reader to understand those words and passages in a particular way. Thus the word *wilderness* became associated with a certain geographical area and also with temptations initiated by the devil. First-century Jews also connected the idea of wilderness with the coming drama of salvation.

The third element involves the Jewish Christians' use of both the Bible and Jewish tradition to explain and defend their faith. The story of Jesus' temptation illustrates how structure in biblical passages betrays the conceptual frame of reference of the people who formulated the story. These people set up the narrative so that each temptation of Jesus parallels a temptation which Israel failed during its wilderness wanderings. In addition, this parallel structure fits a widely accepted Jewish belief of that time: that the age of salvation would in some measure repeat the first age of deliverance from Egyptian bondage.

Thus Gerhardsson's method of analysis enables the modern reader to enter the world of the story. It does not, however, guarantee automatic success in interpreting the narratives of Jewish Christianity. It falls short in several respects. For example, Gerhardsson worked only with specific sentences quoted from the Old Testament (OT); however, Jewish Christians also used individual words and phrases quoted from the OT stories to which they were alluding. A category like "Jewish tradition," furthermore, covers a vast amount of material. Gerhardsson's methodology gives no specific directions concerning which elements of Jewish tradition or which exegetical traditions lie in the background of a particular NT narrative. Here interpreters must be guided by their knowledge of Jewish tradition and by intuition. In seeking to understand the work of the Jewish Christians who formulated the story, the interpreter must still be sensitive to the story's structure, to word usage, and to biblical allusions. Finally, Gerhardsson seems to have applied this methodology only to the narrative of the temptation. The following chapters apply it to three additional narratives.

Having entered the world of the story, we must still address two crucial questions: What is the main thrust or meaning of this narrative? And what does this narrative tell us about the theology of the Jewish Christians who first formulated it? The conclusion of this book brings together the results of each analysis to determine answers to these questions.

Another set of questions, somewhat less crucial but nevertheless compelling, runs throughout the book: What do these stories tell us about the self-understanding of the community which produced them? On the basis of their theology, how did these people perceive themselves? Were they a scholarly community like the community that produced the Dead Sea Scrolls? How did they worship and show their spirituality?

I also consider how each narrative fits into the context—both theological and structural—of the later Gospel that contains it.

One last comment should be added concerning Gerhardsson's "genetic analysis." Although Gerhardsson believes that the temptation story is a Christian midrash, his method of analysis "fits" the formal elements of the narrative. Whether or not the story is a midrash according to a technical definition of that term is still very much a matter of debate. Some scholars even deny the existence of a form called "Christian midrash." What is *not* a matter of debate is the presence of Gerhardsson's three elements. The story does quote several passages from the Hebrew Bible, referred to by Christians as the Old Testament. Also, the same exegetical traditions associated with the word *wilderness* appear in the Dead Sea Scrolls. A number of interpreters have commented on the parallel structure of the story and assigned its formulation to Jewish Christianity. Since this method of analysis is based on elements found within the narratives themselves, it is an adequate instrument for entering into the world of the story and thereby determining its meaning. The claim that a given story is a midrash may or may not be true.

The other methodological issue concerns the dating of exegetical traditions and other aspects of Jewish tradition appearing in the stories. The exegetical traditions found within the temptation narrative pose no questions about dating, because they are the same traditions as those within the Dead Sea Scrolls. Since the community of the Scrolls flourished at approximately the same time that the temptation narrative was written, these exegetical traditions could have been known by Jewish Christians.

The real problem for methodology arises when the NT seems to reflect an exegetical tradition which is otherwise known only from later Jewish works. If such Jewish tradition cannot be dated to the first century, it can hardly be used to illumine the world of the story. In this case I have followed the methodology outlined by Geza Vermes in his book *Jesus and the World of Judaism*.[4] Chapter 1 will discuss this methodology in detail, covering the dating of the targumic material. Here, however, I will simply outline the four possibilities for setting forth the relationship between such a NT passage and a similar exegetical tradition in rabbinic literature that may be dated several hundred years afterward.

First, the similarity may be purely coincidental; second, as Vermes suggests, the rabbinic passage may have "borrowed from" or been "inspired by" the NT. Since the rabbinic passage is chronologically later than the NT, this is theoretically possible, but given the tension between Christianity and Judaism, it is quite unrealistic. A third possibility is that the NT depends on such rabbinic literature as targum and midrash. In this case actual dependence upon targum and midrash presupposes an early date for such rabbinic literature. This, of course, is far earlier than any authority today dates them.

The fourth possibility holds that the NT and the similar rabbinic exegetical tradition "both derive from a common source, viz., Jewish traditional teaching." Here Vermes means that the similar exegetical tradition in question was known in first-century Jewish teaching and later came to literary expression in rabbinic literature. In addition, we do know that certain exegetical traditions continued unchanged for hundreds of years. We are of course assuming with Vermes that the NT is "a witness of first-century Jewish religious thought." Since few serious scholars today would contest such a view, Vermes asks, "[D]oes not this suggested procedure seem methodologically sound and valid?"[5]

Similar to the problem of dating Jewish exegetical traditions is the problem of determining which NT narratives were formulated by early Jewish Christians. Again, the issue of dating is prominent, and the work of other scholars has largely influenced my selection.

The story of the baptism of Jesus is a good example. After a thorough examination of just one motif in the story, Leander E. Keck concludes,

> Specifically, we have ... anchored the story in the earliest milieu in which traditions of Jesus emerged—Palestinian, Aramaic-using Christianity.[6]

Similar research guided my selection of the other stories.

The other criterion influencing my choice of stories was the location of the narrative in chronologically early strata of the NT. The narratives of the baptism, of the feeding of the five thousand, and of the transfiguration all appear in Mark, the earliest Gospel. Further, a scholarly consensus holds that Mark used pre-Markan accounts as sources both for the feeding of the five thousand and for the transfiguration. The source of Matthew's version of the temptation narrative is Q, which is usually dated about A.D. 50. Thus all four narratives date from before A.D. 70. While it is difficult to date the pre-Markan accounts, they likely pre-date Mark by at least several years.

At this point some may ask why narratives yield such a rich theological harvest and why other stories such as miracles—particularly healing miracles and demon exorcisms—and pronouncement stories do not. Did not some miracle and pronouncement stories also arise from Jewish Christianity? Here the form critics can help us find an answer. The two latter forms focus on something that Jesus did or said, while the narratives selected for this book focus on Jesus himself. For example, in the pronouncement story about taxes we learn that Jesus said, "Render to Caesar the things that are Caesar's, and to God the things that are God's" (Mark 12:17). The story shows us that Jesus spoke with authority and that he taught something about taxes. Aside from this, the interpreter learns little about Jesus' role in Jewish Christianity.

One important question remains extraneous to this study. I am not here seeking to get behind a literary account to find out what event in the ministry of Jesus gave rise to a particular story. In short, I am not dealing with the historical question; I am not asking, "What happened?" However, there is a kind of inevitability about the historical question, making it hard to avoid. In discussing the Johannine narrative of the feeding of the five thousand, several interpreters mention that John 6:14 and 15 contain genuine historical information. Moreover, we must not prejudge historical authenticity from the perspective of a twentieth-century worldview. The community of the Dead Sea Scrolls lived in the wilderness so as to withstand the testing of the devil and to keep the law perfectly. John the Baptist lived in the same wilderness. What appears fantastic to a twentieth-century American made good sense to a first-century Jew anticipating the time of salvation. Nevertheless, because the historical question lies outside the scope of this investigation, I attempt only to determine the meaning of the story and to explore the theology it conveys. Accordingly, when referring to those who produced these stories, I use the rather awkward term *formulators* in order to avoid prejudging the historical question by using such terms as *writers* or *creators*.

1 The Baptism of Jesus and the Binding of Isaac

A study of early Jewish Christian theology appropriately begins with the story of the baptism of Jesus, for two reasons. First, this story is today a widely acknowledged literary remnant of Jewish Christianity. It also inaugurates the public ministry of Jesus and is the first narrative about Jesus in the Gospel of Mark.

However, like other such stories, the baptismal narrative presents difficulties for a modern interpreter. Not only is the narrative nearly two thousand years old, but it was formulated by an oriental people whose mindset was quite different from that of the Greeks and Romans, our intellectual ancestors. A second difficulty here is the early Jewish Christians' penchant for referring to the stories they knew so well from the Hebrew Bible. In describing the baptism of Jesus, for example, they recalled their own story of deliverance at the Red Sea in the time of Moses. The Gospel's words of the heavenly voice to Jesus—"Thou art my beloved Son" (Mark 1:11)—also echo God's voice telling Abraham to sacrifice "your only son Isaac, whom you love" (Gen. 22:2) on Mount Moriah.

Modern scholars, understandably snared in these two difficulties, have ascribed to the baptism of Jesus a variety of contradictory meanings. For some, the significance of the event lay in the inner experience of Jesus. They interpreted the occasion as a religious experience that Jesus had, or as a call that he received from God, similar to the calls received by the Old Testament prophets.

Later Rudolf Bultmann persuaded many New Testament scholars to reject interpretations that involve such psychologizing. Asserting that the story reveals more about the faith of the church than it does about the inner experience of Jesus, he classified the story as a "faith legend" which "tells of Jesus' consecration as messiah."[1] Bultmann's messianic interpretation of this story has been criticized, however, because the baptism story lacks the usual messianic expressions. Indeed, Bultmann's view leans heavily on the supposition that the words "Thou art my beloved Son" are a quotation from Psalm 2:7, a royal psalm often interpreted messianically.

In company with other scholars, Alan Richardson has pointed to the parallel relationship between the baptism-temptation of Jesus and that of Israel under Moses:

> As Israel of old, the 'son' whom God called out of Egypt, was baptized in the Red Sea and tempted in the Wilderness, so also God's Son, the Messiah, is baptized and tempted.[2]

Both Richardson and others have read the words of the voice from heaven as "a clear echo of Gen. 22:12" and posited the sacrifice of Isaac as "one of the OT themes which underlie the Synoptic account of the baptism."[3]

This sampling of criticism, while not exhaustive, suggests two observations. On the one hand, the contradictory nature of these views shows that they cannot all be true; but, on the other hand, biblical stories frequently are many-faceted and consequently support a number of interpretations. Nevertheless, the number of varying interpretations raises two questions of fundamental importance for this study. First, what does the baptism story really mean? Does it have one central thrust or interpretation that accounts for its narrative elements more fully than other interpretations do? The second question concerns methodology. How can a modern interpreter enter into the life-world of those who first told and heard the story? Is there a way for us to state the meaning in terms of the story itself rather than reading into it our own preconceived ideas? Let us begin with this latter question.

A Method of Approach

Birger Gerhardsson's method of analysis, as the introduction explains, proposes that these stories be examined in terms of

three elements of which they were composed: words from the Hebrew Bible or Old Testament; Jewish tradition; and the contribution
of the Jewish Christians who formulated the story to express their
faith in Jesus. These three elements, present in this story, enable
interpreters to state the meaning in terms of the story itself.

The Main Thrust of the Story

I believe that the story of the baptism does have a central
interpretation, modeled on the binding of Isaac, the story found in
Genesis 22. However, its immediate background is not so much the
scriptural account of the binding of Isaac as the Jewish tradition that
became associated with that account at the time the NT story of the
baptism was formulated. The story from the Hebrew Bible was not
static and fixed, but continued to grow and develop within the Jewish
community. One of the greatest changes introduced into the biblical
account, for example, concerns the role of Isaac, who played an
increasingly prominent part in the story and even became a kind of
prototypical martyr. In Genesis, the whole significance of the story
lies in Abraham's faith and obedience to God's will. The devout
Abraham is willing to sacrifice his only son, the child of promise;
Isaac himself is a purely passive figure. Jewish tradition, however,
strongly emphasizes the voluntary nature of Isaac's sacrifice.[4] Thus,
when the first-century historian Josephus retells the old biblical narrative, the character Isaac, who is twenty-five years old, rushes to the
altar to be sacrificed:

> The son of such a father could not but be bravehearted, and Isaac received
> these words with joy. He exclaimed that he deserved never to have been
> born at all, were he to reject the decision of God and of his father and not
> readily resign himself to what was the will of both, seeing that, were this
> the resolution of his father alone, it would have been impious to disobey;
> and with that he rushed to the altar and his doom.[5]

A Jew of Josephus' time, hearing the baptismal story, would immediately recall features from the story of the binding of Isaac. In the
account of the baptism, the "images" of the two characters—Jesus
and Isaac—merge into each other. The central thrust of the story is

therefore complex; it tells of the inauguration of Jesus' public ministry, but it also recalls a crucial event in the lives of Abraham and Isaac. Consequently, Jesus becomes associated with a central event in Israel's past.

We are actually dealing here with the history of a tradition—that is, a series of exegetical interpretations that continued to change and develop with the passage of time. The story of the binding of Isaac continued to excite the imagination of the Jewish community, and interpreters continued to seek in the story answers that would address the community's contemporary needs. Some exegetical traditions, such as the kind of symbolic interpretation which equated the term "Lebanon" (wherever it appeared in Scripture) with the temple of Jerusalem, continued unchanged for centuries,[6] but others changed with the addition of new elements. Such changes occurred in the exegetical traditions based on Genesis 22.

While the change away from the biblical story recorded by Josephus is easy to date, other developments in the exegetical traditions concerning Genesis 22 pose problems for comparison with the NT. The primary problem concerns exegetical traditions which seem to be echoed in the NT, but which were first *written* hundreds of years after the NT. While some of these exegetical traditions existed in oral form in the NT period, others had not yet been created. Of course, we must compare the NT accounts with exegetical traditions that, so far as possible, are datable within the first century. However, dating some exegetical traditions is a difficult matter. We will return to the problem of dating at the end of this chapter.

One other parenthetical issue bears mentioning here. Although Matthew, Mark, and Luke contain similar accounts of the baptism, I have selected only the Markan account for comparison with the exegetical traditions based on Genesis 22. Most NT scholars agree that Mark's account was written first and that the other two evangelists are in some measure dependent on his version of the story. Furthermore, if the form-critical study given below is correct, Mark's account more purely exemplifies the form of a vision than does the version found in either later Gospel. And comparing only one account with the Jewish tradition is much easier than constantly noting minor differences between three accounts.

Words from Genesis 22

While most interpreters say that the voice from heaven uttered a sentence composed of phrases from Psalm 2:7 and Isaiah 42:1, a strong minority of NT scholars consider the words "my beloved Son" in Mark 1:11 to be an adaptation of a phrase from the Greek version of Genesis 22, verses 2, 12, and 16. There God refers to Abraham's son, Isaac, as "your beloved son."[7] The phrase "beloved son" is crucially important, but first we must examine the indirect evidence that creates a proper context for discussion.

Significant indirect evidence suggests that the Jewish Christian scribes responsible for Mark's account had Genesis 22 in mind. Apparently never considered before is the fact that among the fifty-three Greek words composing Mark's brief account, there are many astonishing words in common with the Greek translation of Genesis 22. For example, both Mark and the Greek translation (hereafter the Septuagint) open with the same introductory phrase (*kai egeneto*), which the translators of Mark 1:9 have omitted. Also, both use the word "came" near the beginning of the narrative and the word "voice" near the end of the narrative. In perhaps another echo, Mark 1:11 reads "from the heavens," similar to "from the heaven" in Genesis 22:11 and 15. An important word in both accounts is the verb "he saw." Jesus "saw" the heavens being split and the spirit descending. In Genesis 22:4 Abraham "saw" the place, and in verse 14 he names the place "The Lord will see." Certainly, in the development of the tradition recorded in the *Mekilta*, the "seeing" of God becomes the focal point of interpretation.[8] Most importantly, the verb "split," which has so troubled interpreters of Mark's account, appears in both stories. Abraham, "having split" the wood, goes to the place of sacrifice, while Jesus sees the heavens "being split."

These verbal echoes of key terms from Genesis 22 within the short span of Mark's narrative create a remarkable cumulative effect. Note how the story looks when the words in common between Genesis 22 and Mark are underlined. Although Mark replaces the singular "heaven" of the Septuagint with the plural, he uses the word twice in his narrative, as does Genesis 22; he also uses the rare (for him) introductory phrase that the RSV translators of both Genesis 22 and Mark omit in English.

> (9) (*and it happened*) In those days Jesus *came* from Nazareth of Galilee and was baptized by John in the Jordan. (10) And when he came up out of the water, immediately *he saw the heavens opened* [*split*] and the Spirit descending upon him like a dove; (11) *and a voice came from heaven*, "Thou art my *beloved Son*; with thee I am well pleased."

Could this be coincidence?

Now let us turn to the direct evidence that the phrase "beloved Son" is quoted from Genesis 22. The phrase is found within the first half of the sentence spoken by the heavenly voice to Jesus at his baptism: "Thou art my beloved Son." Most interpreters hold that these words are quoted from Psalm 2:7, where God addresses the king of Israel: "You are my son, today I have begotten you." If the words to Jesus are indeed drawn from this psalm, then two difficulties immediately arise: the problematic origin of the adjective "beloved" and the ambiguous meaning of the term "Son" in this context.

Since the adjective "beloved" is not found in Psalm 2:7, some recent interpreters have inferred an influence from the targumic rendering of this psalm. (A targum is an Aramaic translation of the Hebrew Bible.) Marshall, however, citing the uncertain date of the targumic rendering, suggests that the closest parallel for the wording "beloved Son" is the Septuagint translation of Genesis 22:2, 12, 16.[9] Accordingly, the difficulty still stands for those who argue that the words quote Psalm 2:7.

The second difficulty concerns the meaning of "Son": Is it a messianic title and hence to be understood in a purely functional manner? Or is the personal relationship of Jesus to God as his Father the more basic stage of development, as Marshall, Dunn, and others have argued? According to Marshall, the term "beloved" describes Jesus' uniquely personal and filial relationship to God and thereby designates much more than a functional relationship like that of God to a messiah.[10]

Cumulatively, the four points discussed above weigh heavily in favor of the view that Genesis 22 is indeed the source of the phrase "beloved Son." All this evidence—the indirect but significant verbal echoes of Genesis 22 in the text of Mark 1:9–11; the absence of the term "beloved" in Psalm 2:7 and the uncertain date of the Aramaic translation which might supply the term; the presence of the combination "beloved son" in the Greek text of Genesis 22; and finally, perhaps most importantly, the understanding of Psalm 2:7 as a messianic proof-text—and the resultant inappropriateness of "beloved" as a messianic designation—supports the thesis that Mark's account derives substantially from the passage in Genesis.

Now let us turn our attention to the second half of the sentence spoken by the heavenly voice: "with thee I am well pleased." While most interpreters contend that these words are quoted from Isaiah 42:1, I believe that the latter half of this sentence also relies on the exegetical traditions stemming from Genesis 22. Again, two problems confront those who derive the words from Isaiah 42:1. Various interpreters have ascribed these words to a number of sources *other* than Isaiah 42:1; and furthermore, the word for "well pleased" does not appear in the Septuagint of this verse. In fact, the Septuagint uses an entirely different Greek word. Accordingly the argument for Markan dependence on Isaiah 42:1 is weaker than most interpreters commonly suppose.

In arguing that the Jewish tradition associated with Genesis 22 is also the source of the latter half of the sentence, we must begin by defining the key term "well pleased." While the verb comprises a range of meanings, in this context it means "God's decree of election." Here, Jesus is the recipient of God's "elective good pleasure."[11]

Also, in the targums two key terms associated with Isaac convey the idea of election. In three of the targums to Genesis 22:10, the Aramaic word for "unique, only" describes both Abraham and Isaac. This same word designates people who are elected by God. Even more to the point is the use of the term "chosen" in three of the targums to Leviticus 22:27, where Isaac is designated as a "lamb" that "has been elected/chosen."[12]

Perhaps the clearest evidence that both halves of the heavenly voice's sentence came from the Isaac tradition occurs in the book of Jubilees. This Palestinian book, written at least a hundred years before Christ, contains the following sentence addressed to God by Mastema (another name for the devil): "Behold, Abraham loves Isaac, his son. And he is more pleased with him than everything."[13] This amazing parallel presents new evidence: in a Palestinian source that retells the Genesis 22 story, we find both halves of the heavenly voice's sentence to Jesus.

Thus our hypothesis grows stronger. Not only do the words of the heavenly voice derive from exegetical traditions based on Genesis 22, but both halves of the statement come from the same story. Accordingly the messianic and servanthood motifs should not receive primary emphasis in an interpretation of this passage, since they derive from Psalm 2:7 and Isaiah 42:1, respectively.

An exploration of the Jewish tradition lying behind the Markan narrative is the next step in our analysis. The comparison between the Markan narrative and the development of the Isaac tradition recorded in the targums is unique to this study.

The Jewish Tradition: Form Criticism

The Jewish tradition that lies behind Mark may be divided into three parts. We have already seen the main features in the development of Genesis 22 recorded by Josephus, in which Isaac, now an adult, willingly seeks a sacrificial death in obedience to his father's request. A second part is the distinctive literary form that the Markan narrative exemplifies, and the third part involves the parallels and similarities between Mark and that development of the tradition recorded in the targums. Since the Markan account presupposes but does not mention the data recorded by Josephus (Isaac would have to be an adult to be compared with Jesus in any meaningful way), we can dismiss this line of inquiry and focus instead on the literary form of Mark's account, noting the similarities that exist between it and the targumic development of the Genesis 22 tradition.

Fritzleo Lentzen-Deis, the form-critical scholar who has subjected the Markan account to intensive analysis, classifies the story on the basis of such formal elements as the opening of heaven and the voice from heaven. These two elements indicate the form to be that of the "vision," rather than the "theophany" or the "epiphany," as older scholars tended to classify it. The "vision" form is found in the Hebrew Bible, in some of the Jewish literature subsequent to the Hebrew Bible, and in other literature from the ancient world.

However, the targums further develop the "vision" into the related literary form of the *Deute-Vision* (a vision that points out). While the targumic *Deute-Vision* retains the elements of the opening of heaven and the heavenly voice, it focuses on the content of the words spoken by the heavenly voice. These words interpret or point out for the reader the significance of the moment in the life of the person who sees the vision and hears the voice. Lentzen-Deis also shows that the Markan story corresponds exactly to the formal elements that constitute this literary form.[14]

In describing the characteristics of the *Deute-Vision* (hereafter, interpretive vision) for the Isaac tradition, Lentzen-Deis first examines the targumic expansions of Genesis 22:10 and 14. In addition to Genesis 22, he considers Genesis 28:12, Genesis 3:22, and Isaiah 6:6–7. For the Isaac tradition, Lentzen-Deis relies primarily on targum "Pseudo-Jonathan" or Jerusalem I; the "Fragmenttargum" or Jerusalem II; and "Neofiti." He employs the following sigla for these three targums: Tg J I, Tg J II, and Tg N.

In order to understand the form more fully, we should outline the formal elements of the interpretive vision for both stories. Note that the form is characterized essentially by three elements: the opening of heaven (and accompanying vision), the voice from heaven, and the words of the voice. Mark 1:10 describes the first of these very simply: "And when he came up out of the water, immediately he saw the heavens opened." According to the targums to Genesis 22:10, as Isaac lies upon the altar, "the eyes of Isaac" see "the angels of the height." Seeing the "angels of the height" is simply another way of saying that heaven was opened. As the object of his vision, Jesus sees "the Spirit descending upon him." In the targums to Genesis 22:14, Isaac sees "the Shekinah of the Lord" (Tg J I) or "the glory of the Shekinah of the Lord" (Tg J II and Tg N).

As for the heavenly voice, Mark 1:11 simply records that "a voice came from heaven." At this point the targums to Genesis 22:10 diverge. According to Tg J I "the angels of the height respond," while in Tg J II "the angels of the height come and speak to each other." Tg N states that "a voice came from heaven and said."

Mark 1:11 has the heavenly voice speak these words: "Thou art my beloved Son; with thee I am well pleased." In the targums to Genesis 22:10, the wording of the passage is relatively uniform; only the words in common are translated, and the minor differences between the three targums are not noted: "Come, see two chosen individuals (*yachid'in*) in the world: the one sacrificing and the other being sacrificed: the one sacrificing is not hesitating and the one being sacrificed stretches forth his neck." In neither story do the words from heaven explain the vision; rather, the words explain the significance of the scene for the individuals involved and constitute the primary focus of the interpretive vision. Thus the words assure Jesus that he is the chosen/elect Son of God.

The fact that both stories exemplify the same *form* accounts for the similarity in *formal characteristics*. Hence both Isaac and Jesus see a vision and hear a heavenly voice. What is surprising is the similarity of the *contents* within those *formal characteristics*. Indeed, the parallels between the contents of the vision and of the heavenly voice are striking and argue that one story has been modeled on the other. We turn now to the specific developments of the Jewish tradition in these three targums and then draw the parallels between the targums and Mark.

The Jewish Tradition in the Targums

After the opening of heaven, the vision in the targums records either the "Shekinah" or "the glory of the Shekinah." Both Lentzen-Deis and Vermes argue that the revelation of the Shekinah is the oldest version of the tradition,[15] a version which later rabbis abandoned for the longer, less anthropomorphic account.

Ascertaining the precise nuance of the term "Shekinah" is tricky, since the particular meaning sometimes varies with the passage. Fortunately, there seems to be uniform usage within the Tannaitic stratum that lies closest to the Gospels, as Efraim Urbach shows:

> We may sum up as follows: In Tannaitic literature the term "Shekhinah" is used when the manifestation of the Lord and His nearness to man are spoken of.[16]

The term probably carries this Tannaitic meaning because in the context Isaac *sees* something. The targums' other term for God, *Memra*, primarily refers to God's speaking or doing. In these three targums an additional nuance may be present. Since Isaac is lying on an altar on the temple mount, the implication may be the nearness of God *in the temple*. Thus, in this context the term "Shekinah" expresses the "manifestation" and "nearness" of God to Isaac and Abraham on *this* mountain.

Let us briefly review the contents of the message spoken by the heavenly voice. In pointing to Abraham as the one who sacrifices and Isaac as the sacrificial victim, the voice explains the significance of the scene: Abraham and Isaac provide a kind of anticipatory enactment and validation of all the subsequent sacrifices that will be offered in the temple on this mountain. Hence, both Abraham and Isaac are designated by the Aramaic word *yachid'*. The Hebrew form of this noun occurs three times in Genesis 22:2, 22:12, and 22:16 to describe Isaac. While the Aramaic word primarily means "only, single, individual," in these particular targumic passages it also designates those elected by God, as Lentzen-Deis has pointed out.[17]

While the dove is found in Mark's version, but not in the targumic accounts, perhaps Jewish tradition can shed some light on the riddle this dove has posed for all interpreters: why was the Holy Spirit associated with the dove, and what does the dove represent? The dove may be a symbol for Israel.[18] The midrash on the *Song of Songs*, for example, compares the qualities of the dove to the qualities of Israel, commenting on the phrase "Thine eyes are as doves":

> As the dove is chaste, so Israel are chaste. As the dove puts forth her neck for slaughter, so do Israel, as it says, *For Thy sake we are killed all the day* (Ps. XLIV, 23). As the dove atones for iniquities, so Israel atone for the other nations.[19]

Since the same things could be said of Isaac in the light of Genesis 22, is there a possible bridge here to the figure of Isaac and then the story of the baptism?

The dove shares a remarkable characteristic with Isaac: they both stretch forth their neck. We have already met this characteristic in the three targums to Genesis 22:10: "Come, see two unique individuals: . . . the one being sacrificed stretches forth his neck." This characteristic is repeated in *Midrash Rabbah Deuteronomy* 9:4: "What mighty man is there like Isaac who stretched out his neck on the altar?"[20]

Note how these ideas flow together. The dove is an example or token for Israel in that it makes atonement and stretches forth its neck. Isaac, too, stretches forth his neck on the altar as he makes atonement for Israel. It is possible that the dove, *which later was associated with Isaac,*[21] had been associated with sacrifice or Isaac in NT times and consequently found its way into the baptismal account.

Let us now turn to the work of those early Jewish Christians who first formulated this story.

The Work of Early Jewish Christians

Delineating the work of Jewish Christians is much more difficult than simply tracing the Jewish tradition and ascertaining the correct Scripture quotations in the narratives. The difficulty lies in attempting to separate history and theology. On the one hand, it is altogether possible that after his baptism Jesus had such a visionary experience as the narrative describes. On the other hand, Jewish Christians may have added the vision in order to model the story of the baptism after that of the binding of Isaac. If so, they were like the targumists, who "interpreted" Genesis 22 by adding the interpretive vision to the translation of that chapter. While we can only guess what really happened, we may assume that Jewish Christians played a significant role in shaping the brief Markan narrative. This shaping accounts for the striking parallels in both the content and the form of the Markan narrative with the exegetical traditions associated with Genesis 22.

In the vision of Isaac, the term "Shekinah" expresses both the manifestation and nearness of God to Abraham and Isaac on the temple mount. Comparably, in the Markan story Jesus sees "the Spirit," another reference to God's presence.[22] Like the targumic accounts which specify occasion and place for the vision, the Markan account specifies the Jordan River and underlines the significance of the occasion in the words of the heavenly voice. It also points to the temple mount because it emphasizes the much-discussed word "tear" for the opening of the heavens.

Thus the Holy Spirit in the Synoptic accounts functions much like the Shekinah in the targumic accounts. Is it then surprising to find that the two terms were sometimes interchangeable? Arthur Marmorstein explains,

The two expressions are often interchanged in the old rabbinic texts. Both are frequently used as synonyms for God and are so to be interpreted in Tannaitic texts. . . . The man who is closely united with the Shekhinah also possesses the Holy Spirit, and the one possessing the Spirit also sees the Shekhinah.[23]

Furthermore, these two terms share an interesting fluidity of use in their respective stories. Where Luke mentions "Holy Spirit," Matthew writes "Spirit of God" and Mark says simply "the Spirit."[24] This same fluidity occurs in the various accounts of Isaac's vision. Such a flexible use of terms is what we might expect in a Jewish milieu; indeed, it is precisely what McNamara explains about parallel texts:

Rabbinic texts can express the same idea in other ways. In some contexts "the holy spirit" can be replaced by such terms as "the Shekinah," "the Dibbêra" (Word) and "Bath Qôl" (Voice). In point of fact, where in one text we find "holy spirit," in parallel texts we read one of the others, these being more or less synonymous in certain contexts.[25]

The Holy Spirit, then, is as close a Christian equivalent as could be found for the Shekinah of the Isaac story. Given the church's experience with the Holy Spirit, perhaps the Jewish Christians simply exchanged the two terms.

There seems to be no parallel in the targums to the Holy Spirit's *descent* upon Jesus. Does this reflect what really happened, or does it emphasize that Jesus was considered the bearer of the Spirit during his ministry?

If our analysis of the words from heaven in Mark's account is correct, the first half of that sentence quotes Genesis 22 and the second half describes God's "elective good pleasure" in Jesus. In the targums, the words from heaven interpret the significance of Abraham's and Isaac's actions and, by use of the plural of *yachid'*, describe both men as unique/elect individuals. Thus both halves of Mark's sentence are mirrored in the contents of the targumic statements as well as in the account in the book of Jubilees. How does one explain such a striking parallel? Here we see most clearly the work of those Jewish Christians who formulated the story.

Perhaps the most amazing similarity between Mark and the targums lies in the widely accepted form-critical analysis of Lentzen-Deis. The interpretive vision appears characteristically in the targums, and the binding of Isaac is one of the best examples of that form. Mark's account contains that same type of vision. Could early Jewish Christians have known the targumic form unless they also knew the stories that exemplified it? It seems indisputable that they were familiar with the interpretive vision as a narrative form.

One other passage—from outside the targums—can throw light on the Markan text and its targumic parallels. The following lines are from the Testaments of the Twelve Patriarchs, Testament of Levi 18:6–7:

> The heavens will be opened,
> and from the temple of glory sanctification will come upon him,
> with a fatherly voice, as from Abraham to Isaac.
> And the glory of the Most High shall burst forth upon him.
> And the spirit of understanding and sanctification shall rest upon him.[26]

Scholars have long debated whether this is a Christian interpolation into a second-century B.C. Jewish work or a messianic prophecy. If the passage is a Christian interpolation, it explicitly identifies Genesis 22 with Jesus' baptism and proves our point. If it is a messianic prediction, the clear association of Genesis 22 with a scene so similar to Jesus' baptism is still noteworthy, for it argues indirectly that our above assumptions are correct.

The Theological Significance of the Two Scenes

The Fragmentary Targum states quite simply the theological significance of the Isaac story:

> Now I pray for mercy before you, O Lord God, that when the children of Isaac come to a time of distress, You may remember on their behalf the binding of Isaac their father, and loose and forgive them their sins and deliver them from all distress, so that the generations which follow him may say: In the mountain of the Temple of the Lord, Abraham offered Isaac his son.[27]

Unfortunately, Mark's story has no such direct interpretation. Perhaps the place to begin is with the Gospel as a whole. Certainly, most scholars agree that Mark proclaims a theology of the cross; the shadow of that cross falls over most of the Gospel. (Indeed, if our thesis is correct, it falls upon the very first story that deals with Jesus.) Two important words in the Gospel connect Jesus' baptism to the cross. The first receives emphasis in the third prediction of the passion, when Jesus asks his disciples, "Are you able to drink the cup that I drink, or to be *baptized* with the *baptism* with which I am *baptized?*" (10:38, italics added). The second, found within the baptismal account itself, is the word which means split, tear, or open (*schizo*). This term appears again in 15:38: "And the curtain of the temple was torn in two." Rabbis would recognize this connection at once as a *Gezera Shava*, an *"analogy of expressions . . .* based on identical or similar words occurring in two different passages of Scripture."[28] According to exegetical practice, if one of the passages in which the word occurs is obscure, its meaning is to be ascertained from the other passage.

A recent literary study of Mark 15:38 and its context shows the relationship between Jesus' death and the temple in the theology of Mark's Gospel. Harry L. Chronis conveniently summarizes his research:

> Mark 15:37–39 has been shown to be a carefully constructed and theologically intricate passage. In 15:37–39, Mark has creatively woven together the central themes of his gospel to bring the drama to a powerful climax. For Mark, the rending of the temple veil (15:38) is not simply an event signifying divine disqualification of the temple and its cultus. It also functions at an important level in the drama as an interpretive metaphor, phrased in cultic idiom, for both the self-sacrificial character and the self-revelatory force of Jesus' death.[29]

In short, as Chronis states elsewhere, "Mark is seeking to portray Jesus as the replacement for the temple."[30]

Chronis' study suggests three salient points. First, many of the new literary critics today de-emphasize the messianic significance of the title "Son of God/Son" throughout the Gospel and in Mark 1:11. This confirms our analysis of the term "beloved Son" as spoken by the voice from heaven. Second, Chronis' work emphasizes the passive-voice form of "tear" (*schizo*), which ties together 1:11 and 15:38 and points to the significant "tearing" of the temple curtain. This supports our thesis that the baptismal scene, since it is modeled after Isaac's binding on the temple mount, should be understood sacrificially. As Chronis also shows, Mark is a skillful literary artist who reveals his primary theological concerns at the conclusion of his drama[31]; thus we have no explicit interpretation of the baptismal scene, and we can reasonably assume that the scene was modeled on the Jewish development of Genesis 22. Such a merging of Jesus and Isaac, in fact, is typical in Mark, for in his accounts Elijah, John, and Jesus merge into each other, as do Satan and Peter.

The baptismal narrative possesses a double theological meaning. As an element in Mark's Gospel it introduces two of that book's major themes: Jesus' unique relationship to God, and the saving significance of his death. Furthermore, it interprets the vague sacrificial language found in 10:45. But the narrative also functions as an important unit in itself; by paralleling Jesus' baptism with the binding of Isaac, the early Jewish Christians were able to express their new faith through old, familiar terms. As Isaac was the unique/beloved son of Abraham, so Jesus is the unique/beloved Son of God. This typology showed Jesus' relationship to God outside of any reference to a messianic role. Also, by means of this typology, Jewish Christians could explain Jesus' death as a sacrifice for sin.

If this baptismal narrative is typical of early Jewish Christian theological thought, two important observations follow. Christology, or defining the significance of Jesus for faith, was evidently a central concern of Jewish Christians' reflections. The story also reveals much about how these people approached theology—they drew parallels between Jesus and figures from Israel's past. Thus Jewish Christians communicated their theology in story form, and the stories they formulated reflected other stories from the Hebrew Bible.

Dating the Targumic Material

Dating this targumic material is essential for any comparative study involving the NT. Could the exegetical traditions found in the targums have influenced those who first formulated the story of the baptism? Indeed, dating the targumic material is difficult, since the editing of the targums in their present written form took place perhaps hundreds of years after the writing of the Gospels. As in the case of the midrashim, the date of compilation or final editing and the date of composition may vary considerably. The problem of dating targumic material is further complicated by the fact that targums or translations of the Hebrew Bible possibly were known in oral form, perhaps long before they were written.

In view of the complexity of the problem, it may help to stand back from the details and view the possible alternatives before attempting to "solve" the problem. What are the possible relationships between the Jewish Christian narrative of the baptism and the targumic parallels?

The first possibility is that the parallels or similarities are coincidental. Here interpreters would have to say that the *Deute-Vision* evolved from the Old Testament form of the vision both in Mark and in the targums, so that identical elements are retained and the stress falls on the words from the heavenly voice. So also with the parallels found within the formal elements. Clearly, this theory strains credulity. As a second possibility, the targums may have borrowed from Mark. Here the targumists felt that the Markan development of the *Deute-Vision* was a big improvement on the OT vision-form and was ideally suited to present the Jewish development of Genesis 22. Of course, as Vermes points out, to demonstrate that the targumists not only knew the Greek NT story, but also were willing to borrow the form and much of its contents, "is asking a lot."[32] A third—and highly unlikely—possibility is that Mark used the written targums in their present form. Most interpreters believe that this is impossible because the targums, like the midrashim, were not written until centuries after Mark.

We are left, then, with a fourth possibility: that the Markan narrative and the parallels cited from the targums were both drawing from a common source, namely Jewish exegetical tradition that mirrored the developments in the biblical story of Genesis 22. Quite likely the vision-that-interprets and the accompanying elements of that form were transmitted orally in the synagogues, and hence were known by the Jewish Christians who were responsible for the baptismal narrative.

In addition to the above theoretical model, Robert Hayward has argued persuasively that the targumic accounts of the sacrifice of Isaac were extant before the destruction of the temple in A.D. 70. Sometimes such external events provide help in dating passages. The targumic material, for example, locates the binding of Isaac on the temple mount and makes the object of Isaac's vision the Shekinah, which later came to dwell within the temple building. According to Hayward, the emphasis on such data shows that

> the Targums have used Aqedah to prove the sole legitimacy of Jerusalem and its Temple as the place of sacrifice. . . . Such assertions would make good sense in the period before 70 A.D., when the Jerusalem cult was directly challenged by the Samaritans and the adherents of the Temple of Onias at Leontopolis, as well as by the Qumran Sect.[33]

In addition, Hayward argues that targumic material *may* be dated by the presence of similar material in outside sources which *can be* dated. For example, both the targums and IV Maccabees present the death of Isaac as that of a martyr and both regard his death as effective and expiatory. Thus, fixing "the composition date of IV Maccabees . . . at a time antedating the period of Paul's literary activity by at least a decade"[34] shows that the exegetical tradition concerning Isaac's sacrifice in the targums could have been known by and used by the NT writers. Another example of such dating methods is Isaac's *voluntary* submission to sacrifice. The first-century writer Josephus, cited earlier in this chapter, presented this image of Isaac, as did Philo (another first-century writer) and two other first-century documents, IV Maccabees and Pseudo-Philo. Relying on such historical evidence, Hayward holds that exegetical traditions in the targumic accounts of the sacrifice of Isaac were known before A.D. 70.

Conclusions

Following the research of Keck and Lentzen-Deis, this study traces the first formulation of the baptismal story to Jewish Christian circles in the milieu of the synagogue. It maintains that there are probably layers of meaning in the story, which was no doubt formulated in the Jewish Christian church before Mark gave it new narrative functions in his Gospel. Drawing more than one meaning from a story is entirely consistent with a Jewish milieu.

Strong evidence implies that the Isaac-Jesus typology is the main thrust of Mark's narrative. The form is shared by Mark and the targums, and the content shows striking parallels to exegetical traditions in the three targums. The narrative's Jewish Christian origin—the milieu of the synagogue—is also the milieu of the targums. While other interpretations focus on a phrase or a possible quotation from the Hebrew Bible, the Isaac-Jesus parallel is much more comprehensive in its scope. Moreover, it "fits" the theology of the Gospel of Mark and is tied to the temple by means of the word "tear."

2 The Temptation of Jesus

Critical Issues

We have learned that the early Jewish Christians sometimes communicated their theology in narrative form. However, understanding a first-century Christian Jewish story presents particular difficulties, for it involves entering the thought-world of those who told the story. In addition, these difficulties are compounded because the stories formulated by early Jewish Christians were based upon other stories from the Hebrew Bible. Such is the case with the temptation of Jesus, which is based upon biblical stories concerning the wilderness wanderings of the Israelites after Moses led them out of Egyptian bondage.

However, before beginning the formidable task of analyzing the story of the temptation of Jesus, we must address certain preliminary questions, matters of biblical criticism which will influence any subsequent analysis of the story. In the case of the temptation story, these questions concern source criticism and form criticism.

Source criticism is a logical place to begin, since the New Testament contains not just one narrative of the temptation, but three. Source criticism seeks to determine the relationship between these three narratives (found in Matthew 4:1–11, Mark 1:12–13, and Luke 4:1–13) and their source.

In studying the three stories of the temptation, source critics have arrived at a consensus. The Lukan and Matthean accounts are so similar that the authors of these Gospels are thought to have copied them from a common source. Nevertheless, although Matthew's and Luke's accounts are similar, there are also differences, such as the order of the second and third temptations. How does one explain these differences? Which version more nearly reflects the source from which both evangelists copied? Here most critics agree that the Matthean version of the narrative more closely echoes the Q source from which it was taken than does the Lukan. For example, Luke seems to have changed the order of the second and third temptation to suit his theological perspective, while Matthew gives the order of the temptations as Israel experienced them in the wilderness.

While the Matthean account usually takes precedence over the Lukan, the situation is complicated by the presence of a very brief temptation story in Mark's Gospel. Is Mark following a different tradition or an earlier and possibly more historical version of Matthew's and Luke's accounts? Scholars simply do not know. However, since the enigmatic Markan story poses so many questions, interpreters are not sure precisely what the story is saying other than the fact that Jesus was tempted. Consequently, the following discussion will interpret Matthew's account and will not complicate matters by making comparisons between the three accounts in Matthew, Mark, and Luke.

In addition, many contemporary scholars are willing to say more about the origin of the story than the fact that it can be traced to the source used by Matthew and Luke. They believe that the story originated in a Jewish Christian milieu.[1] Not only do the citations from Scripture reflect Jewish practice, but the narrative as a whole reflects Jewish exegetical traditions of the time.

Another critical issue concerns the form of the story. In classifying the stories which compose the Gospels, form critics have been able to agree in describing the parts or elements which constitute the form (or outline) of a parable, a miracle story, or other narrative. However, in attempting to classify the form of this story, form critics have not been able to agree, as a brief review of their efforts will show.

Perhaps, Rudolf Bultmann best represents the discipline in that he could not describe with precision the formal characteristics of the story or its situation in life (place of origin). In his initial description he used the vague term "scribal Haggada." (Haggadah is a broad category of Jewish literature which deals with matters of belief and biblical exegesis. *Haggadah* is always distinguished from *Halacha*, which deals with matters of legal interpretation and standards of conduct.) Two pages later he qualified that earlier description:

The work of Christian scribes made the story in Q and gave it the form of a controversy dialogue on the Jewish model.[2]

On the basis of its form he assigned the story "to the sphere of the Palestinian Tradition" and popularized the phrase "Christian scribes" in reference to the story. On the other hand, he described the phrase "Son of God" as a "Hellenistic concept."[3]

In his recent commentary to Luke, Joseph Fitzmyer classifies the Lukan version of the Q story as a "Story about Jesus, part of the narrative tradition." Apparently Fitzmyer is following Vincent Taylor, who defined a "Story about Jesus" as follows:

Like the miracle-stories, but differing from them in subject-matter, are other stories vivid and colourful in character, but with no distinctive form.[4]

Other recent interpreters, particularly those who work with Matthew's Gospel, have tended to classify the narrative as a Christian midrash.[5]

The temptation story, then, defies easy classification. Perhaps classifying it as a "Story about Jesus" says too little in that such a story has "no distinctive form," yet, the presence of quotations from the Hebrew Bible could be considered a formal characteristic and, as such, is always present in midrash. On the other hand, those who describe the form as a midrash may be saying more than they can prove, since the nature of midrash is itself problematic. While an accurate description of the form of a story does help interpreters establish its meaning, further attempts to work with this story can hardly proceed without a clear definition of midrash itself.

Nevertheless, classifying the form of a piece of literature is important, because form and meaning are closely related. The correct description of a form, such as prose, poetry, or even a scientific experiment, is related to the meaning of that work, since words are used differently in each case. For help in classifying the form of the temptation story, I turn again to the method of analysis proposed by Birger Gerhardsson.

Throughout the following analysis, the words quoted from the Hebrew Bible are all taken from the ancient Greek translation of that Bible known as the Septuagint (LXX). Matthew and Luke wrote in Greek and in writing this story quoted from the Septuagint.

Words from the Greek Bible

In response to the temptations the devil placed before him, Jesus cited three passages from Deuteronomy (Deut. 8:3b in Matt. 4:4, Deut. 6:16 in Matt. 4:7, and Deut. 6:13 in Matt. 4:10). While these citations constitute an important element in the narrative, they refer to more than the words that are quoted. The use of such citations in Jewish exegetical practice sometimes points to the context or surrounding passage from which the specific words were taken. Of course, the broad context of all three proof-texts is the wandering of Israel in the wilderness of Sinai after the Exodus from Egypt. More specifically, the context of Deuteronomy 8:3b is the giving of the manna; that of 6:16 is the incident at Massah where Israel dared to test God by demanding a miracle as proof of divine presence; and that of 6:13 is Moses' warning to the people: "You shall not go after other gods" (Deut. 6:14).

In addition to such typical contextual references, the temptation narrative itself shows that the story's formulators had the context of Deuteronomy 8:3b in mind. The first temptation (Matt. 4:3–4) culminates in the citation from Deuteronomy 8:3b; however, the earlier "setting" of the story (Matt. 4:1–2) also quotes several important words from the immediate context of 8:3b. Thus the Greek words for "was led," "the wilderness," and "tempted" apparently derive from the Greek version of Deuteronomy 8:2. Furthermore, the word for "son" in Matthew 4:3 occurs in Deuteronomy 8:5. Note how words from the context of Deuteronomy 8:3b (and specifically from 8:2) reappear as key words of the setting in Matthew 4:1: "Then Jesus *was led* up by the Spirit into *the wilderness* to be *tempted* by the devil" (italics added). Such repetition of key contextual words was also standard exegetical practice of the time.

Since the writer so extensively used the context of Deuteronomy 8:3b, perhaps he also thought that the purpose of God's testing Israel in the wilderness applied equally to the tests put before Jesus. According to Deuteronomy 8:2, "the LORD your God has led you these forty years in the wilderness . . . testing you to know what was in your heart, whether you would keep his commandments, or not." The forty days of Jesus' temptations indisputably recall the forty-year testing of Israel.[6]

Another verse also deserves consideration here. Deuteronomy 1:1 reads, "These are the words that Moses spoke to all Israel beyond the Jordan in the wilderness, in the Arabah over against Suph, between Paran and Tophel, Laban, Hazeroth and Dizahab." According to a well-known Jewish exegetical tradition, this verse—and especially its first two Hebrew words ("these words")—was regarded as an introduction to the whole book, including such passages as the temptations mentioned in the three proof-texts quoted by Jesus. The exegetical tradition associated with Deuteronomy 1:1 held not only that this verse introduced the book, but also that it represented Moses' words of rebuke or chastisement because Israel had repeatedly failed God's tests. Both aspects of the tradition are clear in the first few lines of Sifrei Deuteronomy, a kind of exegetical commentary on the book of Deuteronomy:

> (1:1) "These are the words that Moses spoke. . . ." Surely Moses did not speak only the words that follow [that is, the rest of Deuteronomy] alone, did he not also write the whole Torah? As Scripture says, "And Moses wrote this law . . . ." What does the verse mean? "These are the words that Moses spoke. . . ." [This verse] teaches that they were words of rebuke.[7]

Accordingly the first verse of Deuteronomy, although it does not appear as a citation in the temptation narrative, sets the stage for the whole book.

The Jewish Tradition: The Dead Sea Scrolls

The exegetical tradition associated with Deuteronomy 1:1 opens an investigation of Jewish tradition lying behind the temptation narrative. This exegetical tradition provided a kind of lens through which the formulators of the narrative interpreted the Scripture passages with which they were working and thereby enabled them to structure the story as they did. We will provide a detailed exposition of this exegetical tradition after first investigating other Jewish exegetical traditions found in the Dead Sea Scrolls.

The Scrolls are a logical place to begin, because the community that produced them was located in the wilderness and was flourishing during the ministry of Jesus—even during the time the temptation narrative was created. Fortunately, the Scrolls provide a helpful summary of the Jewish tradition in areas crucial for understanding the temptation story. Much of the relevant tradition clusters conveniently around the concept "wilderness," which occupies a central place in the thought of the Scrolls. Thus, according to a crucial text found in The Community Rule, the sect went into the "wilderness" to prepare for God's coming act of deliverance:

> And when these exist as a community (13) in Israel, according to this programme they shall be separated from among the settlement of the men of iniquity to go into the desert, to prepare there the way of Him, (14) as it is written,
>
> In the wilderness prepare the way of . . . in the Arabah they shall make straight a highway for our God (Isa. 40:3).
>
> (15) This means study of the Law [which] he commanded by the hand of Moses . . . .[8]

Perhaps the foremost element of tradition associated with the term "wilderness" is geographical: "wilderness" describes the geographical area in which the community was located. Summarizing his discussion of the geographical area designated by the term "wilderness," Robert Funk finds that the NT temptation narratives reflect the usage of the time and particularly the usage of the Dead Sea Scrolls:

> [N]ominal *eremos* [the wilderness] in the NT is usually localized as the wilderness of Sinai or the wilderness of Judea (not just Judah), the latter including the lower Jordan valley and possibly the eastern slopes of the valley. There is precedent for this usage in the LXX and Qumran literature.[9]

Thus the location of the temptations in the NT follows the tradition found in the Dead Sea Scrolls.

Another element of tradition that the term "wilderness" conveys is eschatological. The sect believed that they were living at the end of this evil age and at the beginning of God's new age of deliverance.[10] This eschatological nuance is related to a widespread belief of the time about the activity of God in history: God's actions in one age foreshadow God's future activity. The first congregation in the wilderness under Moses, then, foreshadowed the coming time of salvation. Since the people of the Scrolls believed they were living in the time of salvation and, further, that they stood in some kind of parallel relationship with the generation of Moses, they were in some ways replicating the life of that generation.

The crucial text cited above clearly implies that preparing the way of God in the wilderness meant studying and keeping the law as perfectly as possible. Indeed, the sect's attempt to keep the law of Moses as perfectly as they could introduces yet another element of tradition associated with the term "wilderness." Wilderness means testing. Could the community keep the law as it had been revealed to them? Again, two important passages from The Community Rule teach that the people expected to be tested during the time they were preparing for God's deliverance. In 8:4 The Community Rule speaks of "the endurance of the trial of affliction." And even more importantly, 1 QS 1:16–18 states that the community will be tested during the time that Belial (Satan) rules:

> All who enter the order of the community shall enter into a covenant in the presence of God to act (17) according to all that he has commanded and not to withdraw from following him through any fear or terror or *trial* [i.e., testing, my italics] (18) which take place during the dominion of Belial.

Actually, three aspects of the sect's wilderness-thought appear to be interrelated: "wilderness," "keeping the law," and "testing."[11]

Since this present evil age is under the dominion of Belial, Belial and his followers are responsible for the testing or trials that afflict the "sons of light":

> And by the angel of darkness are the errors of (22) all the sons of righteousness; and all their sins and iniquities and guiltiness and deeds of transgression are in his dominion (23) according to the secrets of God for his appointed time. All their afflictions and the set times of their troubles are under the dominion of his hostility (24) and all the spirits of his portion are set to trip up the sons of light, but the God of Israel and his angel of truth are the help of the (25) sons of light (1 QS 3:22–25).

The community is located in the wilderness "during the dominion of Belial," and thus the wilderness is a primary area of Belial's activity. However, in addition, the association of the demonic with the wilderness is a general idea found in such sources as 1 Enoch 10:4 and Matthew 12:43.

All these associations with wilderness are presupposed in the temptation narrative.

The Jewish Exegetical Tradition

Because scholars have never before associated the exegetical tradition of Deuteronomy 1:1 with the temptation story, and because it answers many questions that have been raised concerning the narrative, this particular exegetical tradition deserves special attention.

The exegetical midrash Sifrei Deuteronomy explicitly identifies the exegetical tradition of chastisement with Deuteronomy 1:1. Furthermore, of the numerous rabbinic works that cite this tradition, Sifrei Deuteronomy seems to stand closest in time to the NT.[12]

Sifrei Deuteronomy explains every one of the place-names mentioned in Deuteronomy 1:1 by showing why Moses had occasion to rebuke the wilderness generation in that place. Several of the place-names receive formulaic treatment. First comes a mention of the *place*, followed by a *formulaic phrase*, and finally the *place-name* is repeated. For example, "'In the wilderness' [the place-name] teaches that he rebuked them concerning whatever they did [formula] 'in the wilderness' [place-name repeated]." Most of the place-names recall a specific story that involves a specific sin. The place-name "in the wilderness" is associated with Israel's complaint preceding the giving of the manna. Sifrei quotes Exodus 16:3, where the people complained, "Would that we had died by the hand of the LORD in the land of Egypt, when we sat by the fleshpots and ate bread to the full." Later, Sifrei cites the incident of the golden calf as Israel's worst sin and associates it with the place-name "Dizahab." Perhaps the earliest rabbinic treatment of this well-known exegetical tradition, Sifrei Deuteronomy also provides the most extensive exposition of it.[13]

The next most important treatment of the tradition appears in the four targums: Neophyti 1, The Fragmentary Targum, Pseudo-Jonathan, and Onkelos.[14] The targums provide important links with Jewish works that were written before the Gospels, and two of the targums reflect a tradition which mentions only three sins of Israel in the wilderness.

These targums to Deuteronomy 1:1 contain little translation in proportion to the amount of explanation: they presuppose the rebuke tradition and "translate" so that the meaning of the rebuke tradition is made clear. Thus three of the four targums incorporate the word "rebuke" into their explanation; only The Fragmentary Targum omits it. All four targums include the incident of the golden calf.

Neophyti 1 and The Fragmentary Targum agree both in listing three wilderness sins as the cause of God's anger, and in naming Israel's three sins: sending out the spies from Paran, grumbling about the manna, and making the golden calf.

The targums also provide important links with Jewish works written before the Gospels. An important link with the book of Jubilees is the mention of the fathers—Abraham, Isaac, and Jacob—in Neophyti 1 and The Fragmentary Targum: greatly angered, God would have destroyed the wilderness generation except for the earlier promise to the fathers. Pseudo-Jonathan refers to the merit of these "righteous fathers," and Onkelos alone is silent on this point. The spies from Paran appear in all the targums except Onkelos, thus furnishing a link with the Damascus Document from the Dead Sea Scrolls.

The targums, therefore, fully explain the rebuke tradition. Two of the targums speak of only three rebukes and agree about them, and the other two do not list as many rebukes as Sifrei Deuteronomy. The targums also bring out the emotional factor in the tradition by focusing on God's anger.

This rebuke tradition is treated with great homiletical skill and beauty in the Midrash Rabbah to Deuteronomy 1:2, where the opening words of Deuteronomy are interpreted by a text drawn from Proverbs 28:23. The Hebrew word for "he who rebukes" interprets "these are the words," and attention is focused upon the incident of the golden calf as the prime example of Israel's failure to be faithful to God. Moses acts in a Promethean role, daring to confront God and attempting to reconcile God and Israel. He tells a parable about a king who became angry with his wife and drove her out of the house. Admonishing Israel, Moses compares Israel to the wife who continues to provoke her husband. Israel, he implies, has provoked God "in the Wilderness, in the Arabah, over against Suph."[15] Evidently Deuteronomy Rabbah also knows of the tradition of the three sins.

Numbers 14:22 brings the rebuke tradition of Deuteronomy 1:1 into an interesting juxtaposition with the tradition of ten trials in the wilderness. This juxtaposition further illustrates the importance of quoting Deuteronomy's words to express the rebuke tradition. The section of the Mishna entitled the "Sayings of the Fathers" (Pirqe Aboth) introduces Numbers 14:22 with these words:

> With ten temptations did our fathers tempt the Holy One, blessed is he, in the wilderness, as it is written [in Numbers 14:22] *Yet have they tempted me these ten times and have not hearkened to my voice.*[16]

The later Talmudic work "The Fathers according to Rabbi Nathan," which serves largely as a commentary on the earlier "Sayings of the Fathers," elucidates the meaning of this Mishnaic passage. It interprets the ten trials by juxtaposing Deuteronomy 1:1 with the sentence copied from the Mishna:

> WITH TEN TRIALS OUR ANCESTORS TRIED THE HOLY ONE, BLESSED BE HE, IN THE WILDERNESS, to wit, In the wilderness, at Arabah, over against Suph, in the neighborhood of Paran and Tophel, and Laban, and Hazeroth, and Di-zahab (Deut. 1:1).[17]

Each of these seven place-names in Deuteronomy 1:1 is then identified with a sin in the wilderness, and three additional place-names from Deuteronomy 9:22 are added. This use of Deuteronomy's words to illustrate the rebuke tradition bears vitally on the interpretation of the NT temptation narrative.

This survey, although it makes no attempt to quote all the rabbinic references to the exegetical tradition associated with Deuteronomy 1:1, nevertheless reveals the strength and variety of its various expressions by citing passages from the Midrashim, the targums, and the Babylonian Talmud. Citations from a Tannaitic work and from the Babylonian Talmud[18] show that the tradition spanned several centuries. For our purposes, however, the crucial problem is tracing the tradition behind the Tannaitic period to NT times and even before the NT was written.

Here, of course, is an important methodological issue. If the exegetical tradition cannot be traced back to NT times, how can an interpreter prove that the tradition influenced the composition of the temptation narrative? On the other hand, if we can prove that a prominent exegetical tradition, familiar in rabbinic literature, was also known in literature of the NT period, then we are virtually assured that NT writers could have known the tradition in question.

Fortunately, evidence shows that the tradition was known both in the Damascus Document of the Dead Sea Scrolls and in the book of Jubilees. In the Damascus Document, column three, we read this rebuke on the wilderness generation:

> And at Kadesh He said to them, "*Go up and possess the land*" (Deut. ix, 23). But they chose their own will and did not heed the voice of their Maker, the commands of their Teacher, but murmured in their tents: and the anger of God was kindled against their congregation.[19]

Two striking points confirm that the author of the above rebuke knew the tradition associated with Deuteronomy 1:1. First, the writer cites Deuteronomy; second, the story alluded to in Deuteronomy 9:23 concerns Israel's sending out spies from the "wilderness of Paran" (Num. 13:3 and 26). Paran is one of the place-names in Deuteronomy 1:1. Also, the story of the spies is one of the causes of God's anger in targum Neophyti 1, in The Fragmentary Targum, and in other passages associated with the rebuke tradition. In "The Fathers according to Rabbi Nathan," for example, Paran is one of the ten "trials" by which the fathers tried "the Holy One, Blessed be He, in the Wilderness."

In the introduction to the book of Jubilees, God speaks to Moses on Mount Sinai before the people have entered the promised land. For the wilderness generation, God has harsh words:

> And you, write for yourself all of these words which I shall cause you to know today, for I know their rebelliousness and their stubbornness before I cause them to enter the land which I swore to their fathers, Abraham, Isaac, and Jacob.[20]

Again, we find two important points of contact with the rebuke tradition. The mention of the fathers recalls this same feature in the rebuke tradition in targum Neophyti 1 and in The Fragmentary Targum. And perhaps even more significantly, the words of the rebuke are a composite of quotations from Deuteronomy 31:27, Deuteronomy 30:20, Deuteronomy 31:20, and possibly Exodus 33:1.

Some evidence implies that the rebuke tradition is known in the NT itself, apart from the temptation narrative. In the book of Acts, Stephen, after telling of the unfaithfulness of the "fathers" in the wilderness, recounts the story of the calf:

> Our fathers refused to obey him [Moses], but thrust him aside, and in their hearts they turned to Egypt, saying to Aaron, "Make for us gods to go before us; as for this Moses who led us out from the land of Egypt, we do not know what has become of him." And they made a calf in those days, and offered a sacrifice to the idol and rejoiced in the works of their hands. (Acts 7:39–41)

Thus the Damascus Document and the book of Jubilees suggest that an early form of the rebuke tradition was known before the NT was written. Perhaps Stephen's speech also reflects knowledge of the tradition, in which the calf is the supreme example of Israel's failure in the wilderness.

In addition, cogent evidence that the scribes who wrote the temptation story knew the tradition is the way in which the rebuke tradition answers questions that modern interpreters put to the narrative.

As so often, Bultmann raises questions which others have glossed over or ignored. In his discussion of the temptation narrative, he comments: "But there is no clue why these three events were told as three temptations of the Son of God."[21] Jacques Dupont, who has taken pains to point out the parallelism between the experiences of Israel and Jesus in the wilderness, suggests that these three temptations were chosen because they are a kind of résumé or summary of Israel's journey in the wilderness.[22] However, Dupont's answer is deceptively simple, because these three incidents emphasize only the negative aspects of Israel's experience. If this is a résumé, why does it overlook the theophany at Sinai and the giving of the law, both central in the rabbinic literature and in the literature contemporary with the NT? One might further ask why only words from Deuteronomy are quoted by the Son of God. For example, in the saying associated with the second temptation—"You shall not tempt the Lord your God"—Jesus might understandably have quoted the primary account of the story, found in Exodus 17:2c ("Why do you put the LORD to the proof?").

Let us proceed in reverse order to show how the questions raised in the previous paragraph find an answer in the rebuke tradition. Why does Jesus quote words only from Deuteronomy? In passages from the rabbinic literature that illustrate the rebuke tradition, the words from Deuteronomy are primary, and the original accounts of the incidents (in Exodus and Numbers) are quoted only to illustrate and to add specificity. Jesus quotes only from Deuteronomy because only these words were regarded as rebukes for Israel's failures.

If one is aware of the rebuke tradition, Dupont's statement is accurate. Thus these three events cited in the narrative may be a summary of the rebukes administered by Moses, but they certainly are not a summary of all Israel's experiences in the wilderness.

In answering Bultmann's query why these three events were chosen to summarize Israel's failures, the exegetical tradition is less clear. While Deuteronomy Rabbah and two of the targums list only three rebukes, "The Fathers according to Rabbi Nathan" mentions ten rebukes. Was the tendency to summarize the rebukes in three incidents known in NT times? However, the rebuke tradition does help answer Bultmann's question. Nearly every text we have read cites an act of idolatry involving either the golden calf or some other incident such as that at Shittim. In addition, almost all of these texts mention the manna in the wilderness. (Given the popularity of this motif in Jewish literature of NT times,[23] we should be surprised by its absence rather than its presence.) Although we do not know what other factors beside the rebuke tradition played a role in the minds of the Christian scribes who wrote this narrative, the rebuke tradition does give answers where previously there was only guesswork and supposition.

The Didactic Activity of Early Jewish Christians

Let us begin this section by making a few general observations about the concept of testing in the narrative. Then we will examine the three temptations individually and conclude by making general observations about the activity of the scribes who compiled the narrative.

In the Hebrew Bible the verb for *test* takes a personal object. Either the people test God, or God tests the people—both individually and as a group. God's classic testing of an individual, for example, is found in Genesis 22:1: "God tested Abraham" by asking him to offer his son Isaac as a burnt offering. In Exodus 17:7 the people test the Lord to prove that He is with them. Such testing of God shows the people's lack of faith; God's testing, on the other hand, is something positive, since testing is the Lord's prerogative. According to Deuteronomy 8:2, God tests Israel in order to "know what was in your heart, whether you would keep his commandments, or not." As Gerhardsson points out, the account of the manna in Deuteronomy 8:1–5 conveys overtones of God's educating and disciplining Israel. When applied to Jesus, then, the temptation is a test designed to reveal what lies in his heart.[24] Here apparently the Jewish tradition and the Christian scribes who compiled the narrative were simply following their understanding of Deuteronomy.

Discussing the Jewish tradition in the Dead Sea Scrolls, we earlier noted the agency of the demonic in testing the "sons of light." The contrast between Genesis 22, and the retelling of that story in the book of Jubilees 17 and 18, shows the development of Jewish tradition on this point. In Genesis "God tested Abraham," but in Jubilees, Mastema suggests the test to God—who in turn puts Abraham to the test. The situation here is somewhat similar to that in the NT, in that both God and the devil are involved in the testing. While the devil actually tests Jesus, God seems to have led Jesus into the tests. According to Matthew 4:1, Jesus was led into the wilderness by the Spirit [of God] in order "to be tempted." The passive infinitive "to be tempted" expresses purpose. In pinpointing God's relationship to the temptations, the scribes were apparently reflecting Jewish tradition. The Scrolls, for example, show that the testing of the "sons of light" by the demonic occurs within the permissive will of God.

Note how Satan initiates the temptation: "If you are the Son of God . . . ." (Matt. 4:3). The devil seems to be calling into question Jesus' Sonship and inviting him to prove it.

What then is the temptation? Matthew 4:2 clearly states that Jesus was hungry after fasting forty days and forty nights. The devil tempts Jesus at the point of his hunger: "If you are the Son of God," prove it by turning these stones into bread. Fitzmyer, observing that "Jesus is challenged to use his power as Son in his own interest," asserts that his answer "implies that Yahweh will supply him with 'manna' once he lifts his eyes beyond desert stones."[25] Perhaps the enigmatic phrase at the conclusion of the narrative is saying that the angels did satisfy Jesus' hunger: "and behold, angels came and ministered to him" (Matt. 4:11).

One thing is clear: the temptation involves the manner in which Jesus will satisfy his own hunger and not that of the people of God. How he alleviates that hunger determines his relationship to God as Son. The question of feeding the hungry people of God, as some would interpret the passage, is entirely beside the point.

The precise nature of the second temptation is much clearer than that of the first, largely because the understanding of Israel's failure at Massah is much clearer. Israel showed lack of faith by challenging God to perform a miracle. According to Exodus 17:7, "they put the LORD to the proof [test] by saying, 'Is the LORD among us or not?'"

By quoting a psalm whose theme is God's protection,[26] the devil tempts Jesus to repeat the lack of faith in God shown by Israel at Massah. "If you are the Son of God," he challenges (Matt. 4:6), then "tempt" God to prove it by performing a miracle for you. The proof-text from Deuteronomy 6:16 exposes the devil's strategy, and Jesus reveals what is in his heart. Again, his relationship to God has been tested.

The third episode makes quite clear the parallel between the temptation of Israel and the temptation the devil puts to Jesus. In the context of Deuteronomy 6:13 Moses warns Israel about idolatry or going "after other gods" (6:14), and in the third temptation the devil openly invites Jesus to "fall down and worship" him. Just as idolatry is one of the typical sins of the wilderness generation (as the rebuke tradition emphasizes), so here Jesus is asked to worship the prince of this world. Idolatry would gain for him "all kingdoms of the world" (4:8).

In addition to the basic parallel between Jesus and the wilderness generation, the Jewish Christian compilers may have been drawing a secondary parallel between Jesus and Moses. The temptation is couched in language that hints of Moses' experience. Moses climbed Mount Nebo "and the LORD showed him all the land" (Deut. 34:1);

similarly, the devil took Jesus to a very high mountain "and showed him all the kingdoms" (Matt. 4:8). The English translation reflects the same Greek words that appear both in the Septuagint and in the NT. Furthermore, the "forty days and forty nights" of Jesus' fast may correspond to the fast of forty days and forty nights by Moses (Deut. 9:9, 18 and Ex. 34:28). Apparently the scribes responsible for the narrative were as fond of secondary parallelism as were later midrashic writers.

Nevertheless, the basic parallelism here is drawn between the temptation presented to Jesus and the temptation of Israel to go after other gods. As before, Jesus turns back the temptation by quoting a passage of Scripture that lays bare the situation. And again, when Jesus' relationship to God is tested, the temptation only disciplines him to reveal a heart faithful and obedient to God.

The first impression one receives from this remarkable artistic achievement is that of its unity. The setting flows as naturally into the first temptation as the first flows into the latter two. The three proof-texts Jesus quotes are all taken from Deuteronomy: they all rehearse events in which the children of Israel failed the tests of the wilderness and thereby reveal a rebellious, unfaithful heart. The parallel between Jesus' faithfulness and the unfaithfulness of the Mosaic generation is subtle and impressive, both artistically and theologically.

Indeed, by parallelling Jesus and the wilderness generation, the early Jewish Christian church formulated a clear affirmation about the way in which it understood Jesus' role as Son of God. Sonship meant faithful obedience to God's will; although the first son was rebellious, this son is obedient. Jesus' faithfulness in the presence of temptation reveals his heart, and thus the narrative's artistic unity conveys an especially lucid theological affirmation. Standing within the Jewish tradition and working with three proof-texts, the Jewish Christian scribes forged a narrative which sturdily voiced their new faith yet beautifully acknowledged their heritage.

Conclusions

A number of modern interpreters have noted the parallel between the temptations of the wilderness generation under Moses and the wilderness temptations of Jesus.[27] Although Jesus relived the temptations of his ancestors, his obedience contrasts with the unfaithfulness of Israel.

The parallel receives considerable depth from the exegetical tradition which regards the words of Deuteronomy 1:1 and other passages as words of rebuke. This tradition emphasized only the negative aspects of the wilderness sojourn, painting it in dark colors, stressing Israel's repeated failures, and often employing emotion. Perhaps the use of this tradition by Jewish Christians reveals some tension in their relationship to the rest of Judaism.

Gerhardsson is surely correct in stating that Jesus' sonship is the focus of the temptations:

> That which is to be put to the test is precisely Jesus' *sonship*; the term *Son of God* is *the key term* in the narrative.[28]

The parallelism between the temptations of the wilderness generation and those of Jesus emphasizes Jesus' faithful obedience in contrast to Israel's lack of it. His obedience demonstrates—rather than earns—his Sonship.

However, while the Sonship of Jesus is the focus of the testing and thereby the point of the story, interpreters do not agree concerning the precise meaning that the appellation "Son of God" conveys. Is it a title for the Messiah? Or does the term, once used to designate God's covenant people as God's son, thereby point to some unique relationship between Jesus and God in a nonmessianic sense? While the narrative itself does not define the term, it offers a cogent reason for choosing the latter interpretation, for it includes no traditional messianic conduct or titles, such as "Christ" or "Messiah."[29]

For further precision in defining the term "Son of God," we can place the temptation narrative in context with the baptismal narrative which immediately precedes it. Alan Richardson argues that the two narratives must be viewed together on the basis of the parallel relationship the two have with the wilderness generation: "As Israel of old, the 'son' whom God called out of Egypt, was baptized in the Red Sea and tempted in the Wilderness,"[30] so also Jesus is baptized in the Jordan and tempted in the wilderness. In view of this tight connection, the meaning of the term "beloved Son" in the one story should cast light on the title "Son of God" in the other story. We have seen that the phrase "my beloved Son" in the baptism does not mean the messiah, but "indicate[s] the unique relationship of Jesus to His Father."[31] Hence, a primary thrust of the narrative shows that Jesus is the Son of God in the sense of a unique relationship to God, as the voice from heaven indicated in the baptism.[32] That unique relationship is demonstrated by obedience and faithfulness under duress.

These two primary conclusions are clarified by pointing to some conclusions that the story is not making. The following paragraphs clarify by way of contrast.

Some scholars, pursuing a different interpretation, see the primary aim of the temptation narrative as catechetical. They believe that the story seeks to strengthen Christians in the tests and persecutions that they face, since the temptations of Jesus are the temptations confronting all people. Did not Saint Paul use the failures of the wilderness generation to warn his own generation? Unfortunately for this interpretation, the narrative clearly compares Jesus to the wilderness generation. The key term is "Son of God," and that term designates Jesus, not all Christians. Finally, nothing in the narrative suggests that the writer(s) had individual Christians in mind, whereas Paul explicitly and repeatedly makes this application.

Other interpreters describe the story as a dramatic creation of the early church, a one-scene summary of the kinds of temptation that faced Jesus in his daily ministry. This may well be true. However, those who propose this interpretation seem to be interested in the origin of the story rather than its meaning. But the question whether the story was created by the early church out of experiences from the later ministry or whether in some way it reflects an actual experience of Jesus is irrelevant here. Again, the meaning of the story lies in its parallelism with the wilderness generation and in the title "Son of God." The story is making a statement about Jesus.

Gerhardsson, who does point to this parallelism, proposes in addition that Jesus was exemplifying the *Shema* (Deut. 6:4ff) in his obedience to God. As the *Shema* tells us to love "God with all your heart, and with all your soul, and with all your might," so each of these ways of loving God corresponds to one of the temptations. Thus loving God with all our soul is the equivalent in the second temptation of testing God's will to save our life.[33] Gerhardsson argues that Jesus must be exemplifying the *Shema*, since the *Shema* is such a prominent theme in Deuteronomy and the contemporary literature and also since two of the temptations refer to the sixth chapter of Deuteronomy, where the *Shema* is found.

Two arguments weigh heavily against Gerhardsson's suggestion. First, no key terms in the narrative indicate that the *Shema* lies in the background. Second, this proposal introduces an additional layer of meaning and thereby forms an alien intrusion into a well-balanced and artistically flawless parallel structure. Gerhardsson would have Jesus' obedience *both* contrast with Israel's disobedience *and* exemplify the *Shema*. The suggestion is forced and unnecessary.

In addition to the two main conclusions discussed above, the narrative also points to a view of history whereby the Mosaic age in some ways would foreshadow, or parallel, the coming time of final deliverance for God's people. This belief is mirrored in numerous passages in the rabbinic literature, in the Dead Sea Scrolls, and in the NT Accordingly, the community of the Scrolls reproduced in its life certain institutions and features of the wilderness age. In a similar vein, Saint Paul in 1 Corinthians 10:1–11 cites the failures of the wilderness generation as a warning to the saints "upon whom the end of the ages has come" (1 Cor. 10:11). Both the community of the Scrolls and Saint Paul believed they were living at the end of the age. Thus the temptation narrative hints that Jesus, the Son of God, is bringing to completion and fulfillment the history of Israel. Moreover, his obedience and faithfulness have in some sense broken the power of the devil. Thus his baptism and temptation herald the time of deliverance.

The view of history whereby one generation sounds the themes that will be repeated on a higher level at the end of the age is the theological presupposition implicit in the narrative itself. The creator(s) of the narrative articulated theology by drawing parallels with Israel's past; here they draw a negative parallel with the wilderness generation. Elsewhere, as we have seen, the baptismal narrative draws a positive double parallel with the patriarch Isaac: Isaac is Abraham's beloved/unique son, and Jesus is God's beloved/unique Son. As the binding of Isaac is a sacrifice for sin, so modeling the baptism of Jesus after the binding of Isaac points forward to the sacrifice of Jesus for the sins of the world.

3 The Feeding of the Five Thousand

Critical Issues

The narrative of the feeding of the five thousand, although not specifically treated by Gerhardsson, lends itself easily to Gerhardsson's method of analysis. However, before investigating the crucial elements of this narrative—the words from Scripture, the Jewish tradition behind it, and the particular contributions of its Jewish Christian formulators—I want to address several critical questions that influence the analysis of the story. Since the feeding of the five thousand is the only miracle from Jesus' Galilean ministry that is found in all four Gospels, the relationship between those four accounts must be examined. There may even be six accounts, because Matthew and Mark both contain a similar story involving the feeding of four thousand people. Further, both Mark and John are widely thought to have used a pre-Gospel story in writing their accounts; if they did so, their redactional changes in those sources are important considerations. Such critical questions make impossible any detailed solution within an introduction of this length. The point of this introduction, however, is not so much to solve critical questions *per se* as to prepare for the analysis of the feeding miracle. Consequently, a brief review of the present scholarly consensus concerning these critical questions and then a brief statement of the bearing of this scholarly consensus on the following analysis are all that can be accomplished.

Perhaps the place to begin is the widely held observation that John's version of the feeding of the five thousand is independent of the accounts found in the Synoptic Gospels. In his exhaustive analysis of the six feeding narratives in the Gospels, Raymond Brown has concluded that John's story is not dependent on the Synoptic accounts.[1] A second widespread consensus among scholars is that Mark's Gospel was written first, and that both Matthew and Luke depend upon Mark's version. Hence, my analysis will devote attention primarily to the accounts in Mark and John rather than those in Matthew and Luke. Third, many scholars believe that the authors responsible for both Mark and John depended upon two pre-Gospel sources while writing the accounts now found in those Gospels. This theory helps explain both the similarities and the differences between the Johannine and Markan versions.

How did these four separate accounts arise? Simply put, an event in the Galilean ministry of Jesus inspired two apparently similar but independent pre-Gospel stories. The author of Mark used one of these stories, and the author of John followed the other. Since Mark's account was in turn used as a source by Matthew and Luke, the pre-Gospel story behind Mark becomes, so to speak, the grandfather of Matthew's and Luke's accounts.

Separating the pre-Gospel source from the Gospel writer's additions to it is the work of redaction criticism. Today, for example, most redaction critics hold that verses 6:30 through 6:33 are entirely or almost entirely the work of Mark, who wrote them to introduce the account of the feeding. Also, verse 34 is largely (but not entirely) Mark's own, though he made other additions *within* the pre-Gospel source. A significant part of my analysis will focus on Mark's introductory verses.

In addition to the narrative of the feeding of the five thousand, found in each of the four Gospels, both Matthew and Mark record another story describing the feeding of *four* thousand. What is the relationship between these two narratives? While there is no scholarly consensus on this issue, many critics believe that the two feeding stories are "doublets" of the same event. Thus Vincent Taylor contrasts the "vivid character" of 6:35–44 with "the more colourless form" of 8:1–10. Bultmann points out that while the stories are "constructed . . . alike," the feeding of the four thousand is, for the most part, "secondary."[2] A more recent and probably more correct view holds that Mark found in the tradition the story of a feeding, and then intentionally created a second feeding story out of it so that his

Gospel would contain two feeding stories.[3] Therefore, since the feeding of the four thousand seems to be a Markan creation and since the feeding of the five thousand reflects a pre-Markan source, I will confine my analysis to the latter story.

This more recent view holds yet another implication for our analysis of Mark 6:35–44. According to this view, the creative work of Mark, which is evident in the redactional verses 30–33, cannot be neatly separated from the rest of the story, because the same characteristics of Markan style and literary technique appear throughout both feeding narratives. Consequently, in analyzing 6:35–44 it is not possible simply to assign certain words to Mark and other words to his source.

While scholars agree on most of the critical issues discussed above, they are divided in classifying the *form* of this story. Like the stories of Jesus' baptism and temptation, the feeding of the five thousand inspires assorted classifications. Although Bultmann, for example, defines the narrative as a "nature miracle,"[4] it is unlike most other miracle stories of Jesus in two respects: the disciples participate in it, and it lacks the typical awe-filled response of the crowd (and/or disciples). Martin Dibelius, seeing in this story the symbolism of the Lord's Supper, classifies it as a "Tale." The miracle, he asserts, points beyond itself to the significance of the miracle worker:

> The Feeding of the Five Thousand also contains an epiphany [an appearance of the divine on earth], not, of course, to the 5,000, but to the Christian readers. Again, without reference to the origin of the material, we may sense the deeper meaning of the picture as painted by the writer: "He looked up to heaven, blessed and brake the loaves, and gave to the disciples." It is the Savior who dispenses the Lord's Supper.[5]

While Dibelius is correct in his reference to the Lord's Supper, the eucharistic symbolism is not the only symbolism found here; nor, as I shall argue, is it the most basic level of symbolism in the story.

Some recent writers, focusing on the epiphanic character of Mark's miracle accounts, emphasize the divine or godlike quality of Jesus' activity and therefore classify the two feeding narratives as epiphany stories.[6] Unfortunately, the tendency to classify more and more stories as epiphanies has stretched the category so widely that the traditional criterion for defining the classification (namely, an appearance of the divine on earth) no longer has any precision. Consequently Fitzmyer, in discussing the Lukan account, perhaps most adequately describes the "form" of this story as "a symbolic miracle in the Synoptic tradition."[7] A symbolic miracle is one which points beyond itself to someone or something else and thus is similar to the signs in the Johannine tradition.

Perhaps John's account can help illustrate the implied symbolism in Mark's narrative. Certainly, in John's Gospel the symbolism implicit in the feeding of the five thousand becomes explicit in the sermon which both follows and interprets the miracle. According to the sermon (John 6:31–58), the miracle symbolizes the manna, the eucharist, and Jesus himself. Further, Ernst Bammel finds in this miracle a symbol of the wilderness wanderings. Discussing verses 14 and 15, which conclude John's miracle story, Bammel writes:

> We encounter a picture of the Feeding according to which the event was such that the imagery of Israel in the desert impressed itself on those present, and did so to such a degree that people felt bound to see in Jesus the antitype of those events.[8]

At this point it is appropriate to outline our thesis and then conclude this introductory section of the chapter by briefly arguing for it.

I believe that the basic symbolism in the Markan account focuses on the manna tradition. The symbolism is implicit in the Markan account because that story is being modeled on an earlier story, as the baptism of Jesus is modeled on the binding of Isaac. Mark's narrative, patterned after the story of the manna in Exodus 16, repeats key words and scenes from that chapter. Thus the central thrust of the NT narrative is complex because it comprises several levels of meaning. While it tells of Jesus' feeding hungry people in a wilderness place, it also recalls a central event in the wilderness wanderings of Israel. Further, the NT story does not simply recall the OT story. The story of the manna was not static and fixed in the Jewish community, but continued to grow with additions. One such addition taught that in the time of deliverance the people of God would again eat manna; the feeding, therefore, signals the arrival of that time. Finally, the eucharistic motif is a natural addition to the story, since the feeding continued to be recounted during the eucharistic celebrations of the church. The narrative thus associates some event in the ministry of Jesus both with the story of the manna, as it was interpreted in Jesus' day, and with the eucharistic life of the church.

Many interpreters would reject the above thesis, finding no implicit reference to the story of the manna in Mark's account of the feeding. Would anyone ever have looked for such an implicit reference in Mark's account if John had not made an explicit identification with manna in his account? Could not the reference to manna be a late addition to the pre-Gospel story by the evangelist John himself? If Mark wanted the feeding of the five thousand to recall the giving of the manna, then he should have made some kind of explicit reference to it. All these objections, though valid, are easily satisfied.

First, demanding that Mark make an explicit identification between the feeding and the manna is simply asking Mark to think and write like John. As Howard Kee has pointed out, Mark's method is quite different from John's; instead of making direct statements, Mark frequently confines himself to more subtle suggestions:

> Mark, in keeping with his esoteric outlook, not only does not go that far but gives only tantalizing hints to his reader of the real meaning of the miracle of feeding.[9]

An even more cogent reason for *not* identifying the bread of the feeding with the manna is advanced by Quentin Quesnell. After a thorough examination of the numerous usages of bread/breads in Mark's Gospel, Quesnell concludes that the word "bread" conveys more than one level of meaning.[10] An explicit identification with any one level of symbolism, therefore, would hinder the term from conveying other levels. For example, if Mark clearly equated bread with the eucharist, it could hardly convey any other meaning.

Although it does lack such explicit connections, the Markan narrative contains numerous hints of Israel's wilderness period. Two examples will suffice. The first is the arrangement of the crowd by hundreds and fifties as they receive the bread, an organization which recalls that of Israel in the wilderness (Exod. 18:21). This same organization is found among the Qumran sectaries who consciously imitated Israel's organization in the wilderness. A second example is

Jesus' compassion for the crowd because they were "like sheep without a shepherd" (Mark 6:34). Moses, having learned of his impending death, asks God to appoint a new leader so that Israel will not be "as sheep which have no shepherd" (Num. 27:17).[11]

As a final refutation to potential objections, Mark's account also furnishes details that underline the connection with the giving of the manna to Israel. Perhaps the most obvious detail is the twice-repeated phrase "to a lonely [wilderness] place" in Mark 6:31 and 32,[12] since "wilderness" is a key term in Exodus 16. Nevertheless, the full significance of this detail is apparent only in context with other details that point to the manna story. The wilderness place, for example, is reached only after Jesus and the "apostles" cross the sea (Mark 6:32). Note the parallel sequence of events in both scenes: Jesus and the disciples cross the sea to the wilderness place, and then the hungry five thousand are fed; in Exodus the Israelites cross the sea, wander in the wilderness, become hungry, and are fed with manna. Mark also gives two additional details that characterize Exodus 16. Although Mauser (see note 11, above) associates the theme of rest with the wilderness wanderings in general, the Exodus narrative connects with sabbath observance *two* main themes: the tradition of rest, and the eating of the manna. Mark mentions both rest and eating in verse 31.

The cumulative effect of these four details is enhanced by the fact that they all occur within Mark's redactional verses. Today most NT scholars agree that an author's purpose and theology are most likely found in the redactional passages of a Gospel; accordingly, Mark's details clearly point the reader to the story of the manna.

Another possible parallel with the giving of the manna is the doubling of the feeding stories in Mark's Gospel. While Exodus 16 describes the giving of manna and quail, Numbers 11 contains a second description of the manna and an additional reference to the quail. Although a modern scholar would see a different literary source behind the Numbers account, this explanation would not be available to a first-century writer. These two separate sources may well be the explanation for Mark's accounts of the feeding of the five thousand and then of the four thousand.

One further parallel with the manna is found in 1 Corinthians 10:1-4 where Paul equates the eucharistic bread with the manna by referring to the "supernatural food" which Israel "ate" in the wilderness. Note the equations with which we are working. Mark and John and most likely the pre-Gospel sources they used equated the eucharist with the wilderness feeding; Paul equated the eucharist with the manna. Paul's casual connection, made as if it were already an exegetical tradition, implies a similar equation between wilderness feeding and manna.

Instead of asking Mark to make an explicit identification with the manna, modern scholars might better ask a more realistic question: what knowledge of the Scriptures would the hearers of Mark's Gospel bring to the story? Austin Farrer suggests the following:

> Here are thousands of men faint with hunger in desert places, no apparent means of feeding them, and the disciples in utter perplexity. We cannot but be reminded of the predicament of Moses in the wilderness.[13]

Given the hints and details that Mark supplies, would not a first-century audience (who lived out of the Scripture in ways we do not) arrive at much the same conclusion?

In addition to the lack of an explicit reference to the manna story, the reference to fish causes problems for other interpreters. What do fish have to do with manna? Do the fish not destroy the parallelism between the two stories? The problem with the fish may be approached in either of two ways: either they are an actual historical reminiscence or they are a redactional addition by Mark. Let us first examine the possibility that the fish were actually eaten. Since fish was a staple in the diet of Galileans, and since both John and Mark mention fish, the fish are probably a factual detail. They did not prevent John, however, from drawing a parallel between the feeding and the giving of the manna. Indeed the fish, like the bread, may have carried more than one layer of meaning. In the second story concerning the manna and the quail in Numbers 11, Moses also mentions fish: "Or shall all the fish of the sea be gathered together for them, to suffice them?" (Num. 11:22). Both OT accounts contain the manna and the quail; if on one level the bread symbolizes manna, may not the fish symbolize quail? Farrer confirms this possibility: "Bread and fish, then, is a fair analogy to 'manna and quails.'"[14]

On the other hand, the fish may be an addition to the pre-Markan feeding story by Mark himself. In his critical investigation of Mark's feeding narratives, Paul J. Achtemeier comments on "the intrusive nature of the mention of fish" and consequently ascribes the fish to Markan redactional activity.[15] If the fish were added by Mark, they too might convey more than one level of meaning. W.D. Davies, in fact, suggests that the fish might complement the manna symbolism associated with the bread. Referring to the feeding of the five thousand, he writes:

> This also has undertones of the New Exodus motifs since manna was food for the Messianic meal of the future in Jewish expectation along with Leviathan (which *may* be represented in the fishes of Matt. xiv.17, etc.).[16]

Of course, Mark may also have added the fish as an analogy to the quail, as mentioned above. In neither case, whether the fish are a historical memory or a redactional addition, are the fish an alien intrusion to the manna symbolism.

Finally, since Mark makes no explicit reference to the manna story, some interpreters point to the narrative of Elisha's feeding the two hundred in 2 Kings 4:42–44 as the model for the feeding of the five thousand. Certainly, the two stories have noticeable points in common. Both record the number of loaves and the number of men to be fed, and both emphasize the leftovers after the feeding. In addition, they share basic words like "give," "loaves," and "eat." However, there are differences as well. While Elisha feeds two hundred with twenty loaves, Jesus feeds thousands. Also, the feeding of the five thousand takes place in a wilderness setting, while the other feeding does not. Yet another difference involves the nature of the miracle: there the NT story is unlike both OT counterparts. Although the manna is given in abundance with the dew, without any activity on Moses' part, Elisha himself commands the man from Baalshalishah with the twenty loaves and ears of grain to "Give to the men, that they may eat" (2 Kings 4:42). The story does not explain how the twenty loaves fed two hundred; the reader possibly thinks in terms of analogy with the widow's cruse of oil. In Mark 6:41, on the other hand, the multiplication of the loaves and fishes is modeled on the eucharist: Jesus blessed and broke the loaves and gave them to the disciples to distribute. As Farrer explains,

The number of whole loaves never becomes any greater than it was at first, but each loaf breaks into a number of substantial pieces which are together many times the mass of the unbroken loaf. . . . it is related not to Old Testament types, but to . . . eucharistic custom.[17]

Is the feeding of the five thousand patterned after 2 Kings 4:42–44 or after Exodus 16? It may not be a case of either/or, but both/and, for a story or passage of Scripture may easily have more than one referent. As we have seen, the baptism of Jesus is modeled on the binding of Isaac, and the juxtaposition of the baptism with the wilderness temptations recalls Israel's passing through the sea and subsequent wilderness trials. Thus the baptism story echoes two types from the Hebrew Bible. In the narrative of the feeding, there may be an attempt to say that Jesus is greater than Elisha. Nevertheless, the above paragraphs and the number of words in common between the NT feeding story and its two OT counterparts clearly suggest that the manna story is the primary type.

Aside from the many hints and parallels that connect the story of the manna to the feeding of the five thousand, the most compelling reason for identifying these two stories is their common vocabulary. The Markan version seems to have quoted a significant number of Greek words from the Septuagint account of Exodus 16 (and possibly even Numbers 11). The following section will explore the vocabulary links between Mark 6:30–44 and the story of the giving of the manna.

Words from the Greek Bible[18]

Before considering individual words that the Gospel accounts quote from Exodus 16, it is helpful to examine two possible patterns in which the words are placed. One of these is clearly evident in a sermon from John 6, which explores the meaning of the feeding miracle by combining words from Exodus 16:4a and Exodus 16:15. In verse 4a the Lord says to Moses, "I will rain *bread from heaven* for you" and in verse 15b Moses explains to the people that the manna "is the *bread* which the LORD *has given* you *to eat*."

Two characteristics[19] of this first-century sermon immediately become apparent: key words from the Exodus text are repeated and explained throughout the sermon; and the same key words—"bread" and "from heaven"—cited at the beginning of the sermon in John 6:31, recur at the end in 6:58 to form an "inclusion." In addition the word "bread," perhaps the most important word in the text, is quoted twelve times within the body of the sermon, and the phrase "from heaven" appears seven additional times. A third characteristic is the switch from direct speech to third person narrative. In Exodus 16:15, for example, Moses identifies the manna as the "bread which the LORD has given *you* to eat," and in John 6:31 the word "you" is changed to "them." Two additional characteristics (to be addressed later) involve paraphrasing words from the text and quoting words from the passage surrounding the text.

While these five characteristics constitute the pattern or form of this first-century sermon, they are not confined to sermonic material. For example, the practice of inclusion was frequently used by biblical writers to indicate that a story or unit of thought had been completed, since our highly developed system of punctuation had not yet been invented. I call attention to this pattern because Mark uses some of these same characteristics in telling his version of the feeding of the five thousand. For example, he employs words from Exodus 16:15 as if they were a text and uses the word "eat" to form an inclusion.[20] To a lesser extent Matthew and Luke reflect some of these characteristics. Again, the following analysis does not appear elsewhere in scholarly literature.

The verse in which Moses identifies the manna as "the bread which the LORD has given you to eat" has two echoes in Mark 6:37: in 37a Jesus tells the disciples: "*You give* [them]. . . *to eat*," and in 37b the disciples ask: "Shall we go and buy two hundred denarii worth of *bread*, and *give* it to [them] *to eat*?" Then, as if these words were his text, Mark repeats them during his narration. "Bread" appears four times outside the "text" cited in 6:37, for a total of five citations; "eat," cited twice in verse 37, recurs in verses 31, 36, 42, and 44; and "give," which occurs twice in verse 37, also appears in the eucharistic formula of verse 41.

Verse 37a shows the switch from direct speech to third person. The dative of the pronoun "you" in Exodus 16:15 changes to the dative of "them," as in John 6:31. Then "you" becomes the subject as Jesus commands the disciples to feed the people: "You give them . . . to eat." In addition to repeating these words from the "text," Mark uses the word "eat" to form an inclusion by tying together the introduction (verse 31) and conclusion (verse 44) of the miracle story.

Indeed, the difficulties some interpreters have with the disciples' reply in Mark 6:37b is an indirect witness that a "text" is being repeated. While Taylor comments on the "boldness of the querulous question," a more recent commentator cites the repetition in the verse as a sign of Markan redaction.[21] Whatever the cause, repeating the words of the "text" causes an awkwardness that can only be deliberate.

Note how the pattern looks in the following excerpt from Mark 6:31 through 44, in which the recurring words from Mark's "text" in 6:37 are italicized. Verses 32–34, 39–40, and 43 have been omitted because they contain no words from the "text."

> (31) And he said to them, "Come away by yourselves to a lonely place, and rest a while." For many were coming and going, and they had no leisure even to *eat*. . . . (35) And when it grew late, his disciples came to him and said, "This is a lonely place, and the hour is now late; (36) send them away, to go into the country and villages round about and buy themselves something to *eat*."

> (37) But he answered them, "*You give* them something to *eat*." And they said to him, "Shall we go and buy two hundred denarii worth of *bread* [*loaves* in Greek], and *give* it to them to *eat*?"

> (38) And he said to them, "How many *loaves* have you? Go and see." And when they had found out, they said, "Five, and two fish." . . . (41) And taking the five *loaves* and the two fish he looked up to heaven, and blessed, and broke the *loaves*, and *gave* them to the disciples to set before the people; and he divided the two fish among them all. (42) And they all *ate* and were satisfied. . . . (44) And those who *ate* the *loaves* were five thousand men.

This pattern of quotation and repetition, so noticeable in Mark, is less obvious in Matthew and Luke. Both Matthew and Luke omit the repetition of the "text" in 6:37b, but they copy word for word its first expression in 37a. Also, while Matthew and Luke do repeat the words of the "text," they repeat them less frequently than does Mark. Matthew, after citing the word "eat," repeats the word only twice, and Luke repeats it only in verse 17. Neither Matthew nor Luke forms an inclusion with the word "eat."

Nevertheless these Gospels give additional evidence that Mark quotes Exodus 16:15 when he uses the word for "bread" or "loaf." Both Matthew 14:15 and Luke 9:12–13 show that other words for food were available besides the term Mark consistently uses in this passage. John, too, shows a ready alternative; in the sermon which follows the miracle story, he uses a completely different word for "eat" in both 6:54 and 56. Mark's Gospel contains only the precise term found in Exodus 16:15.

The other pattern of word placement relevant to this study appears in Mark 6:31–32 and was evidently created by Mark. Nearly all scholars agree that he wrote verses 30 through 33 as an introduction for the feeding story which follows them.[22] A chiastic arrangement, the pattern is described by the formula a, b, c, b′, a′:

a = "by yourselves,"
  b = "to a lonely place,"
    c = verse 31b and verse 32a
  b′ = "to a lonely place," and
a′ = "by themselves" (In Greek, words same as *a*).

While the purpose of this pattern is to call attention to *c*, in this instance *ab* and *a′b′* seem to be as important as the material inserted between them. In describing these chiastic phrases, John Dominic Crossan writes: "It has been noted that when Mark makes a redactional insert he very often copies the final expression which his source had before the insertion and after the addition as well."[23] The "final expression" before the redactional insert is b′—"to a lonely place" (more literally, "into a wilderness place"). I suggest that Mark was using Exodus 16 as his source in creating the formula, and that consequently the words "wilderness" and "place" derive from that chapter. In Exodus 16 "wilderness" is a key term, occurring five times—functioning each time as a noun and three times as the object of the same preposition that Mark uses in his formula. Because the word "place" appears only in Exodus 16:29, it is (to quote Crossan) the "final expression" from Mark's source.

Before turning to the material that Mark has inserted within the brackets b and b′, we should note the emphases that follow the word "place" in Exodus 16:29. Verse 30 tells that "the people rested on the seventh day," verse 31 describes the appearance and taste of the manna, and verse 32 contains the combination of key words: "the bread with which I fed you [Greek, "you ate"] in the *wilderness*."

Compare these three emphases with the three found within Mark's redactional insert. Immediately after the bracketing formula in 6:31, Jesus orders the disciples to *rest*; the noun form of Mark's verb for "rest" also occurs in Exodus 16:23. Then Mark tells the reader that "many were coming and going," and that "they had no leisure even to *eat*." In Exodus 16:32 the "bread" which the people *eat* is the manna. The word "eat" occurs seven times in Exodus 16, five of which refer to eating manna. Also, recall that the word "eat" forms an "inclusion" within Mark's account and is repeated six times within his brief narrative. The third emphasis within Mark's brackets is the movement of the disciples and Jesus by boat to the wilderness place (6:32).[24] Crossing the sea to a wilderness place also draws a parallel between Jesus and the wilderness generation, as was noted above.

What does the similarity between the first two emphases of Mark's redactional insert and the emphases following Exodus 16:29c suggest? In addition to using Exodus 16 as his source in creating the bracketing formula, Mark was likely redacting the main emphases within chapter 16 for his insert. Since the main emphases of that chapter are summarized in the verses following 16:29, Mark began redacting after the word "place" and concluded with the word "wilderness" from 16:32c. These two words form the "final expression" before the insert and after it as well. Mark thus reminds his first-century readers of the manna and its related narrative.

In addition, individual words within Mark's pattern derive from Exodus 16. "Wilderness" (or "lonely") "place," "rest," and "eat" have already been mentioned. Mark's next sentence, however, also tells us that the disciples had no leisure "to eat," "for many were coming and going." The word for "coming" is found twice within Exodus 16 (at the beginning and at the end of the chapter), and both times "the people of Israel" is the subject of the verb.

Thus all three elements in the pattern of this insertion technique— the final words of the brackets b and b′ ("to a lonely place"), all three emphases within Mark's insertion, and finally, the vocabulary— strongly suggest that Mark was consciously alluding to the story of the manna in Exodus 16.

Again, underlining the words in common between Mark's redactional insert and Exodus 16 makes clear their connection and significance. Since Mark used the verbal form of the noun "rest" in Exodus 16:23, the line under this verb is broken.

> . . . by yourselves to a lonely place, and rest a while. For many were coming and going, and they had no leisure even to eat. (32) And they went away in the boat to a lonely place by themselves.

Other redactional verses in Mark also suggest that their author was aware of the typological relationship between the manna miracle and the feeding of the five thousand. Verse 30, which forms a transition between the sending out of the twelve and Mark's introduction to the feeding miracle, has been ascribed to Mark on the basis of its vocabulary.[25] Actually, the scene of the twelve disciples' return to Jesus seems to reflect the scene portrayed in Exodus 16:22: after gathering the manna on the sixth day, "all the leaders of the congregation came and told Moses." Again, note the vocabulary. The Greek verb for "returned" (in Mark 6:30) is used twice in Exodus 16 for gathering manna, and its noun form occurs in 16:22. This noun, translated "congregation," appears seven times within the chapter as a title for Israel. As the leaders "told" Moses, so the disciples "told" Jesus; the same verb and tense, except for the initial preposition, occur in both scenes. As "all" the leaders came, so the disciples told Jesus "all"—in fact, "all *that* they had done and taught." In the Greek, the word for "that" is repeated, as is true in the following verse in 16:23. Mark 6:30 contains the verb "had done"; in Exodus 16:17 the identical form of that verb describes the obedience of "the sons of Israel" to God's word. In the entire Markan scene, only the words for "apostles," "to Jesus," and "taught" are absent from the Exodus chapter. If Mark is *not* quoting Exodus 16, this is a remarkable series of coincidences. Appropriately italicized, Mark's redaction in 6:30 reads, "*The* apostles *returned* to Jesus, *and told* him *all that they had done and* [*that*, as added in the Greek version] taught."

Since verse 33 tells that the crowd arrived at the site of the feeding before Jesus and the twelve and thus has nothing to do with the story of the manna, it contains only one verbal allusion to Exodus 16: the word "knew," which will be discussed with verse 38, below. Almost all of verse 34, however, is redactional.[26] Here Mark establishes vocabulary links with the Exodus passage and possibly refers to Moses when he mentions the shepherd. The first two verbs in 6:34a are both found in Exodus 16, each occurring three times. While the verb "to see" is quite common, it is twice used for seeing the manna. The source of the observation that the crowd were "like sheep without a shepherd" has long puzzled commentators. Was Jesus alluding to Numbers 27:17, to Ezekiel 34:5, or to some other passage? Numbers 27:17 refers to Moses as a shepherd, and the manna tradition reinforces this identification: accordingly, Moses is the shepherd who leads the sheep to manna.[27]

In studying Mark's subsequent verses, scholars have had difficulty separating the traditional underlying story from Mark's own redactional comments. Some elements, however, clearly point to Exodus 16 and to the wilderness period during which Israel ate manna for forty years (Exod. 16:35).

Verse 35 seems to contain three references to Exodus 16: the comment of the disciples, the repeated mention of the late hour, and the use of the verb "came to." The disciples' remark, "this is a lonely [wilderness] place," is repeated by Matthew and Luke. The mention that "it [the hour] grew late" may be a paraphrase of the word "evening" from Exodus 16, verses 6, 8, 12, and 13. Exodus 16:13, in fact, couples with "evening" the same verb that Mark joins with "hour." Also, Numbers 11:9 states that: "When the dew fell upon the camp in the night, the manna fell with it"; accordingly, the late hour would appropriately coincide with the falling of the manna. And as the disciples "came to" Jesus (a phrase found also in Matthew and Luke), so in Exodus 16:9 Moses commands the people of Israel to "Come near before the LORD, for he has heard your murmurings." The word for "round about" in Mark's verse 36 furthermore recalls the manna-bearing dew "round about the camp" in 16:13. (See also Num. 11:31 and 32.)

We have already seen that in verse 37 Mark twice repeats the words of Exodus 16:15. The only other vocabulary link is the common verb "he answered," which is found fourteen times in Exodus 16. In nine of these repetitions Moses is the subject, and the verb form is identical.

In verse 38 the use of the word "knowing" (and also the use of the same root in 33a) probably reflects the importance of this verb in Exodus 16, where it twice refers to the knowledge of God. Both times, it occurs in association with bread (manna). According to Exodus 16:12, the people of Israel are filled with bread before they know God: "you shall be filled with bread [manna]; *then* you shall *know* that I am the LORD your God." In Mark the disciples *know* how much bread there is before the miracle takes place. Another important connection is the awkwardness of the expression in which the participle "knowing" occurs. The RSV paraphrases, "when they had found out," and both Matthew and Luke omit the expression.

Three vocabulary links also point to Exodus 16. Jesus asks, "How many *loaves* have you? Go and *see*"; the disciples, "knowing," reply, "Five, and *two* fish." The identical form of "see" is found in 16:29, and its verse continues: "The LORD . . . gives you *bread* [loaves] for *two* days." This juxtaposition of three identical words—"see," "loaves," and "two"—argues persuasively that Exodus 16:29 and Mark 6:38 are joined by more than coincidence.

Verses 39 and 40 should be considered together, because the allusion to the wilderness generation belongs with the vocabulary links. In Mark 6:40 most commentators see a clear allusion to the wilderness generation under Moses, for the people sat down "by hundreds and by fifties." Exodus 18:21 contains this same organizational pattern.

In verse 39—"Then he commanded them all to sit"—two vocabulary links with Exodus 16 are the words "all" and "commanded." Exodus mentions the word "all" eight times; in seven of these, it modifies "the congregation of the people of Israel." In Mark the word "all" designates the Jewish crowd of five thousand. The word "commanded" (the same root, but with a different prepositional prefix) occurs in Exodus four times: God commands three times, and Moses once. Just as the Lord and Moses commanded "all" the congregation in the wilderness, so here Jesus commands "all" the crowd of Jews.

Since the language of verse 41 is eucharistic, we should expect few allusions to Exodus 16. Nevertheless, Mark's reference to heaven in 41b (which is not found in his account of the Last Supper in 14:22) probably reflects the words of Exodus 16:4: "I will rain bread *from heaven* for you." Indeed, the heavenly origin of the manna is a prominent motif in the manna tradition. The repetition of the word "all" at the end of Mark's verse may also echo the repetition of that word in Exodus 16.

Mark 6:42—"And they all ate and were satisfied"—is repeated verbatim by Matthew and Luke. The verse may be quoting Deuteronomy 8:10, which describes the satisfactions of the promised land and, significantly, appears within the Deuteronomic account of the giving of the manna in 8:3–16. However, Exodus 16:8, which speaks of "flesh to *eat* and in the morning bread [manna] to the *full*," is the more likely source. It not only contains the essence of Mark's sentence, but also accounts for the word "all"; just two verses back, Moses addresses "all the people of Israel." In either case, the Greek word for "were satisfied" is not a quotation, but it may be a paraphrase of a word from Exodus 16:8.

If Mark is quoting Exodus 16:8 (or even Deuteronomy 8:10), he or his source may be using a common exegetical technique known as *Gezera Shava*. This is "an *analogy of expressions*, that is, an analogy based on identical or similar words occurring in two different passages of Scripture."[28] Accordingly, if one of the passages containing the words is obscure, its meaning can be ascertained or clarified from the other passage. All the words found in Mark's "text" (derived from Exodus 16:15) are also found in Exodus 16:8. In addition, the words "to the full" (or "were satisfied," in the paraphrase) appear in verse 8. The clarifying information supplied by the *Gezera Shava* is the fact the people involved ate until they were satisfied or "to the full." Research on first-century sermons shows that the words of a text could be paraphrased, and here one Greek word in the LXX is paraphrased by another word with the same meaning. Does this extension of the text by *Gezera Shava* account for the fact that Matthew and Luke copy these words exactly as they do the words of the "text" in 6:37a?

Two words echo Exodus 16 in Mark 6:43, where the disciples "took up twelve" baskets full. The verb for "took up," plus a prepositional prefix, brackets the account of the manna in Exodus 16:1 and 17:1; there, all the congregation "take up" camp and move. Taking up the broken pieces may recall gathering the manna, for in the Johannine account the same verb for gathering the manna is twice used for taking up the broken pieces. While everyone knows the symbolism applied to the twelve baskets here, the number *twelve* also immediately precedes the story of the manna in Exodus 15:27, when the people camped by "twelve springs of water." This kind of numerical coincidence continued to delight later composers of midrash.

Finally, in verse 44 two words from Mark's "text" in 37 are repeated, and the verb "ate" forms an inclusion with the word "eat" in 31. The emphasis on "men" (males) in this story might further echo Exodus 16, which repeats so often the formula "all the congregation of the sons [Greek] of Israel."

The foregoing analysis calls attention to the words that both Mark and his pre-Gospel source "quoted" from Exodus 16. In addition, the Markan account specifically uses words from Exodus 16:15 (or possibly 16:8) as if they were a "text." The words in common between the Exodus chapter and Mark's account tend to be key words in both narratives; furthermore, they significantly dominate Mark's account.

Once more, a diagram will show how many words Mark's account in 6:35–44 shares with Exodus 16. Words in common are underlined, including verbs to which a different preposition is prefixed. References to the wilderness generation are underlined with a broken line.

> (35) And when it grew late, his disciples came to him and said, "This is a lonely place, and the hour is now late; (36) send them away, to go into the country and villages round about and buy themselves something to eat." (37) But he answered them, "You give them something to eat." And they said to him, "Shall we go and buy two hundred denarii worth of bread, and give it to them to eat?" (38) And he said to them, "How many loaves have you? Go and see." And when they had found out, they said, "Five, and two fish." (39) Then he commanded them all to sit down by companies upon the green grass. (40) So they sat down in groups, by hundreds and by fifties. (41) And taking the five loaves and the two fish he looked up to heaven, and blessed, and broke the loaves, and gave them to the disciples to set before the people; and he divided the two fish among them all. (42) And they all ate and were satisfied. (43) And they took up twelve baskets full of broken pieces and of the fish. (44) And those who ate the loaves were five thousand men.

All these words in common, plus the allusions to the wilderness generation and possible paraphrases of words in Exodus 16, create an impressive cumulative effect.

This intricate interplay of words and scenes from Exodus 16 within the Markan account is characteristic of later midrashic writers. One of the best examples of this technique appears in Genesis 18, Abraham's encounter with the three angels. While the passage must be read in Hebrew to appreciate fully the interplay of words and scenes between Abraham's hospitable acts and God's rewards for that hospitality, the following selection illustrates the technique:

> Thus what Abraham did for God, God did for the children of Israel in the desert. Abraham brought water, and so God gave water to the people to drink through the rock in the desert. Abraham served bread, and the people received manna, bread from heaven. Abraham escorted "the three men" down toward Sodom, and so God went with the people in the pillars of fire and cloud.[29]

Not surprisingly, the Abraham/wilderness episodes and the manna/ feeding episodes show similarities in this technique.

Since it is difficult to determine whether Matthew and Luke were aware of the relationship between the feeding stories and the manna story, their accounts have little relevance here. John's narrative of the feeding miracle, however, deserves at least brief mention. We have already seen that in John's Gospel the sermon which follows the miracle (6:31–58) makes an explicit identification with the manna story and uses a text based on Exodus 16:4, plus words from Exodus 16:15. John, following a pre-Gospel source, also quotes from that OT chapter. For example, in the Johannine account the word for "bread/ loaves" is repeated five times, and the word "gather up," which in Exodus 16 is twice used for collecting the manna, here twice describes the gathering of leftover pieces. Strikingly, the identical word and form which God speaks in 16:16 appears as Jesus' command in 6:12: "Gather up." The words for "sit," "eat," "test," "know," "each," "get," and "their full" are common to both stories.

From this lengthy analysis we can draw several conclusions. Certainly John was aware of the relationship between the feeding miracle and the manna miracle, and most likely Mark was too, because both authors interweave words and a text from Exodus 16 into their accounts. Furthermore, the pre-Gospel sources behind John and Mark also must have been modeled on Exodus 16; it is improbable that both evangelists independently arrived at the same typology and approx·

imately the same text. These Markan and Johannine narratives, based on words from the Bible, also reflect the influence of Jewish tradition.

The Jewish Tradition

Since the manna story was apparently popular, the interpreter finds a wealth of exegetical material. Thus the task at hand is to sort out those aspects of the manna tradition that pertain to the feeding miracle as well as those that can be dated to the first century of our era. Dating is not such a problem here as in previous chapters, however, because several recent studies show which parts of the manna tradition were already known in the first century.

As early as the first century of our era, for example, the manna could signal the new age. Many believed that in the age to come manna again would be eaten. Perhaps the clearest expression of this belief is found in Second Baruch, which is dated around A.D. 100:

> And it will happen at that time that the treasury of manna will come down again from on high, and they will eat of it in those years because these are they who will have arrived at the consummation of time.[30]

A similar teaching is found in Revelation 2:17. To the church at Pergamum, John the seer gives this message: "To him who conquers, I will give some of the hidden manna." While the word "hidden" has given rise to several interpretations, the most probable is that the word "hidden" means kept in reserve for those who enter the world or age to come.[31] Of course, as the context in Second Baruch makes clear, the belief in the return of the manna is related to a view of history in which the time of the messiah (or of the final deliverance) will be like the time of the first deliverance under Moses.

Manna was associated not only with the age to come, but also with the Passover. Mentioned, of course, in the Passover Haggadah, manna also appears in Joshua 5:10–12 as a part of the last Passover kept by the Israelites before they eat the produce of the promised land. In fact, Passover, manna, and the bread of the promised land are brought together in this passage. While the Gospel of John may be reflecting Jewish tradition when it associates the feeding of the five thousand with Passover and the eschatological manna,[32] it may also be recording correct historical information.

Another strand within the tradition spiritualizes the manna. Even in the Hebrew Bible some of the manna passages, particularly Deuteronomy 8:3, used the manna to represent religious and moral teaching. This spiritualizing tendency continues in the work of Philo, who equates manna with Logos, wisdom, and Torah. The Mekilta, Exodus 13:17, also equates manna and Torah.[33]

Furthermore, the figure of Moses looms larger in the traditions about the manna than it does in the biblical narratives. According to Pseudo-Philo, *LAB* 20:8, God gave the manna to Israel "on account of" Moses:

> And after Moses died, *the manna stopped* descending upon *the sons of Israel* . . . . And these are the three things that God gave to his people on account of three persons: that is, the well of the water of Marah for Miriam and the pillar of cloud for Aaron and the manna for Moses. And when these came to their end, these three things were taken away from them.[34]

Indeed, in Josephus "the manna descends in answer to Moses' prayer, and the dew which produces it first congeals about his hands."[35]

The later tradition, that Moses himself provided the manna for the people and fed them, may be datable to the first century. The sermon that explains the feeding of the five thousand ascribes these words to Jesus: "it was not Moses who gave you bread from heaven: my Father gives you the true bread from heaven" (John 6:32). This remark seems to presuppose the audience's belief that Moses gave the manna. On the basis of a rabbinic formula which says "Do not read this, but that," Borgen finds that this is precisely what John 6:32 means.[36]

According to John 6:14–15, the five thousand who have been fed proclaim Jesus as "the prophet who is to come into the world!" They then seek "to make him king." After an exhaustive search of the traditions lying behind this "prophet-king" of John 6:14f, Meeks comes to the following conclusion:

> It has now become quite clear from rabbinic as well as non-rabbinic sources, that in some circles of Judaism over an extended period of time, from at least the second century B.C. until the middle ages, Moses was regarded as Israel's ideal king as well as prophet. In isolated traditions the two titles were found closely connected, as the basic offices of Moses.[37]

While the manna tradition is far more extensive than the above passages indicate, these aspects of the tradition seem to illumine the feeding stories.

The Work of Early Jewish Christians

In discussing the contribution of the Jewish Christians who first formulated the story, we must reckon with the possibility that their contribution was based on actual events in the ministry of Jesus. A growing number of interpreters hold this opinion. Among them is Raymond Brown, who comments on John 6:14–15 as follows:

> We believe that in these verses John has given us an item of correct historical information. The ministry of miracles in Galilee culminating in the multiplication (which in John, as in Mark, is the last miracle of the Galilee ministry) aroused a popular fervor that created a danger of an uprising.

Brown further argues that "the invention of the information in vss. 14–15 seems out of the question,"[38] and that the Passover setting for the feeding of the five thousand is probably historical.[39]

Consequently, it is entirely possible that the actual crowds who followed Jesus first associated the feeding with the manna story. However, whether the earliest reflections on the meaning of the feeding came from the crowds who participated in the event or from Jewish Christians, the fundamental symbolism associated with the story seems to be the giving of the manna in the wilderness.[40]

Converting the manna story into a new narrative surely involved more than quoting words from the old story in the new. The Jewish Christian formulators apparently saw the fundamental typology between the manna and the bread as the center of wider circles of parallels that correlated the time of Moses with the time of Jesus. Thus they probably saw a correlation between the nation Israel and an eschatological Israel that was called into being by Jesus' ministry. The organization of the five thousand "by hundreds and by fifties" (Mark 6:40), as mentioned earlier, points to an eschatological community patterned after Israel in the wilderness under Moses. The manna, as a sign of the new age, is eaten by that new community.

The identification of Jesus with the prophet-king or Moses figure belongs to the wider circle of types associated with the manna. It is not clear whether Jesus' withdrawal to the mountain is meant to deny this identification with the prophet-king or simply to deny the time and manner in which the crowd was seeking to make him king.[41] Probably the Jewish Christian formulators of the story approved this identification, although their approval may be obscured by the theology of the evangelists who redacted the pre-Gospel accounts.

A further parallel lies in the miraculous nature of the two events. While modern form critics may not agree whether the story exemplifies the precise form of a miracle story, few would deny that the Gospel writers thought they were recounting a miracle. The same may be true for the pre-Gospel accounts used by Mark and John. Also, while the "J" version of the story in Exodus 16:13b–15 may not be particularly miraculous, other Pentateuchal layers and other versions of the story within the Bible most definitely are. As the story grew, so did its miraculous additions.

All four versions of the feeding of the five thousand contain, in addition to the manna symbolism, eucharistic formulas that appear to be drawn from early liturgies. Were these eucharistic formulas added by the Gospel writers, or did they exist in the pre-Gospel versions used by Mark and John? Apparently, the eucharistic motif dates from these pre-Gospel versions. Both Paul Achtemeier and I. De La Potterie, though approaching Mark's account from different perspectives, conclude that the eucharistic motif of the narrative is pre-Markan.[42] De La Potterie, in fact, argues that the eucharistic motif is the second stage in the history of the pre-Gospel account, since the fundamental episode was seen in the light of the giving of the manna (see note 40). Since a eucharistic emphasis appears both in John 6:11 and in the sermon which follows, particularly verses 51–58, it probably existed in the pre-Gospel source for John's Gospel.

The presence of a eucharistic emphasis within the pre-Gospel versions opens the possibility for establishing a situation in the life of the church in which the account lived for at least some portion of its history. Achtemeier makes the following suggestion:

[A]t some point prior to Mark, the stories of the feeding had their locus in a liturgy accompanying a eucharistic celebration, either as an auxiliary to it, or as part of the catechism accompanying it, the point of which was to clarify the meaning and import of that celebration.[43]

Certainly, the eucharistic emphasis flows naturally from a story of breaking bread in the wilderness, even when that bread symbolizes the gift of manna.

The pre-Gospel accounts behind Mark and John, then, contain eucharistic symbolism and manna symbolism; they are also quite possibly the source for the Passover setting and the attempt to make Jesus a king. Brown's study, cited earlier, claims that the Passover setting in John's account is probably historical. Two details in Mark also point to a Passover setting. Mark's reference in 6:39 to the "green grass" (paralleled in John 6:10 by the statement "there was much grass in the place") may suggest Passover, since green grass grows in the wilderness only in springtime. Furthermore, upon this grass the people sat down "by companies"—an expression which, as Samuel Lachs remarks, may point to the Passover meal.[44]

The attempt to make Jesus a king also finds some notable echoes in the Markan account. As the crowd in John 6:15 attempted to make Jesus king, "Jesus withdrew again to the mountain by himself." Those same Greek words for "mountain" and "by himself" appear in Mark, not at the end of the feeding narrative, but at the beginning of the story of Jesus' walking on the water, which immediately follows the feeding story. (In both pre-Gospel versions the walking on water comes just after the feeding of the five thousand.) At the beginning of Mark's account of the walking on water, Jesus "made" ("forced" would be a better translation) the disciples leave in the boat; after they left, Jesus "dismissed" the crowd and then went up "on the mountain [by himself—a detail not translated into English] to pray." Mark gives no explanation for Jesus' forcing the disciples to leave. De La Potterie argues that the urgency with which Jesus disperses the disciples, and his subsequent withdrawal to the mountain, are best explained by the attempt to make him king (John 6:15).[45] The appearance of the exact Greek words for "mountain" and "by himself" in the same context in both Gospels suggests that although Mark must have known the pre-Gospel explanation for Jesus' mysterious action, he deliberately omitted it.

Since Jewish Christians conveyed their theology in narrative form, a close look at the constituent parts of the story helps us understand what these formulators were trying to say. The theological thrust of the story is implicit in the above analysis; by purpose and design, it presented to its first hearers a very specific message.

The Theological Significance of the Story

The Jewish Christians' penchant for drawing parallels between the time of Jesus and events from Israel's past, evident in the previous chapter, is no less applicable to the feeding of the five thousand. Like the stories discussed earlier, this narrative contains "types" furnished by the generation under Moses.

Implicit in this typological method of doing theology is a view of history that other stories share. As Gärtner says so succinctly, "The salvation of the people out of Egypt is the pattern for the coming salvation."[46] Thus the time of Jesus and his immediate followers is the time of the eschatological fulfillment and salvation. Or as Paul writes in 1 Corinthians 10:11: "Now these things . . . were written down for our instruction, upon whom the end of the ages has come." This view of history and its related narrative method characterize the theological significance of the feeding story.

From the analysis of the work of Jewish Christians we concluded that the basic parallel or type to the feeding of the five thousand is the giving of the manna in Exodus 16, and that that Exodus story was mediated to the Jewish Christians through contemporary exegetical traditions. One such tradition held that in the age to come manna would be eaten again; thus this wilderness manna was equated with the eschatological manna of the age to come. The repetition of the giving of the manna in the wilderness signified that the eschatological age was at hand.

In addition to representing the eschatological manna, the feeding in the wilderness was made to symbolize the eucharist—a possible situation in life of the church for the survival of this story. If, as seems likely, the eucharistic symbolism was also the work of Jewish Christians, the story reveals aspects of their understanding of the eucharist. The sequence of thought from bread in the wilderness to eschatological manna to eucharist implies a strong connection between the eucharistic bread and the manna of the new age. This close relationship, in turn, shows that the eucharist was understood typologically. Therefore it should not be surprising that this same correlation of ideas occurs in 1 Corinthians 10:1–4, where Paul equates the eucharistic bread with the manna and draws the same typology with the "supernatural food" of "our fathers," which they "ate" in the wilderness.

The feeding story has yielded three theological motifs: the view of history that the time of Jesus is the eschatological time of salvation; the understanding that those who eat the eschatological manna are those who have come to the end of this age; and the implication that the eucharist, like the manna, is understood eschatologically.

Note how these three beliefs all help to define the self-understanding of the community that formulated this story and cherished these beliefs. The Jewish Christians saw themselves as an eschatological community living both in the time of salvation and in some kind of typological relationship with the generation under Moses, while they were being fed by the eschatological sacrament. Truly, as Paul says in describing the community at Corinth, they saw themselves as those "upon whom the end of the ages has come."

Although the basic typology was between manna in the wilderness and bread in the wilderness, the Jewish Christians also apparently drew a typological relationship between Moses and Jesus. This relationship is evident in John's account, and less so in Mark's. A minor detail illustrates the difference between the two accounts. In John 6:11 Jesus himself distributes the bread to the people, whereas in Mark 8:6 Jesus gives the loaves to the disciples who in turn distribute them to the people. This Johannine detail fits well with John 6:32, which suggests that Jesus' audience or John's readers believed that Moses gave the manna to the people. As Moses gave manna to the wilderness generation, so Jesus gives the eschatological manna (and eucharistic bread as well) to this generation. The subsequent reaction of the crowd confirms this reasoning. After the feeding, the crowd hails Jesus as "the prophet who is to come into the world" (6:14). Note how closely Meeks identifies this prophet with Moses: "At every point evidence has accumulated for connecting the 'prophet-king' of

6:14f with the tradition of a prophet like Moses."[47] Also, if Bammel is correct, parts of verses 14 and 15 of John 6 were found originally in John's pre-Gospel source.[48] On the other hand, Mark seems to have omitted the typological relationship between Moses and Jesus that his pre-Gospel source probably included. What Mark omitted from his source, John reproduced.

Since both Mark and John emphasize Jesus' religious teaching— Mark in 6:34 and John in the sapiential parts of the sermon in 6:31– 58—it is tempting to suppose that something in the pre-Gospel accounts suggested this emphasis. It could be related to the prophet-like-Moses theme or to the spiritualized understanding of manna whereby manna designated religious and moral teaching. In either case the emphasis on Jesus' teaching is not alien to the manna/Moses typologies.

While Mark does not emphasize the prophet-king aspect of Jewish Christian Christology, he may be deriving his emphasis on teaching in 6:34 from another aspect of the manna/Moses typology. Note that Moses was called the shepherd of Israel (see note 27, above). In the largely redactional verse 34 Jesus has compassion on the Jewish crowd of five thousand because "they were like sheep without a shepherd." Mark gives the episode a christological interpretation: Jesus is the shepherd of the people because he teaches them.[49]

Both themes—the shepherd and religious teaching—may be related to the Moses/manna themes of the pre-Gospel accounts. When he so skillfully composed the introductory verses in 6:30–34, could Mark have shaped this christological episode to harmonize with the main themes of the passage *and of his Gospel?*

Two observations will suffice to establish this story's theological import. First, as contemporary research has shown, the manna tradition was both thriving and popular in first-century Jewish and Jewish Christian circles. While central to the interpretation of this story, the manna tradition in Deuteronomy 8:3 also lies behind one of the three temptations of Jesus in the previous story. Further, the popularity of the manna tradition is related to the popular view of history whereby the wilderness generation under Moses furnished "types" for the eschatological time of salvation.

The second observation is that an important contrast exists between the primary theological thrust of this story and that of the two previous stories. In those two narratives, the theological reflections of the Jewish Christians focused on the role and significance of Jesus for their faith. Here, however, the christological reflection is not only secondary but also somewhat muted. If Paul is any guide here, the manna motif, especially when joined with the eucharistic emphasis, necessarily involves a community. Thus Paul writes that the experience of "our fathers" constitutes a warning "written down for *our* instruction" (1 Cor. 10:11). Additionally, the prophet-king aspect of the Moses/Jesus typology was not the primary way in which either Mark or John conveyed his message about Jesus. In the sixth chapter of John, in the sermon, Jesus exalts himself at the expense of the manna; he draws a contrast between himself and "the manna in the wilderness," describing himself as "the *living* bread which came down from heaven":[50]

> Your fathers ate the manna in the wilderness, and they died. . . . I am the living bread which came down from heaven; if any one eats of this bread, he will live for ever. (John 6:49, 51a)

Finally, we must depart from the theology of Jewish Christianity in order to understand how the typology is compatible with the theology of Mark and of John, and how it contributes to their theology and purposes. The feeding of the five thousand fits admirably into Mark's overall eschatological outlook; along with the feeding of the four thousand, it performs a very specific function in his Gospel. The five thousand were Jewish, and the event happened on Jewish soil. Thus, in Kelber's words, "on the western side of the lake the Markan Jesus constitutes the Jewish part of the Kingdom." How, then, does Mark use the feeding of the *four* thousand? Kelber maintains that "after the 'Gentile issue' is resolved, Jesus designates in a second feeding on the eastern side what can only be the Gentile part of the Galilean Kingdom" (8:1–10).[51] The eschatological feedings, then, designate the inclusion of both Jews and Gentiles into the eschatological kingdom of God.

The feeding of the five thousand also constitutes an integral part of John's Gospel. The first half of this Gospel is built around signs that point to the deeper importance of Jesus. Before the episode of the man born blind, for example, Jesus calls himself "the light of the world" (John 9:5) so that his statement may clarify the sign that follows. The feeding is another sign which identifies Jesus. Here, John contrasts Jesus with the manna: "your fathers ate [it] . . . and they died." Jesus alone, he states, is "the bread which comes down from heaven, that a man may eat of it and not die" (6:50). Although Mark and John make different uses of the story, in both Gospels the feeding of the five thousand contributes to those evangelists' particular theology and purposes.

Although Mark and John treat this narrative differently, they do not seem to have distorted its meaning. The story, as it was formulated by Jewish Christians, was perhaps initially associated with the eschatological manna, and later with the eucharistic beliefs of the church. While Mark emphasized the story's eschatological thrust, John focused on its eucharistic and sapiential aspects to further his aim of realized eschatology.

Many contemporary scholars believe that the feeding of the five thousand was originally an anticipation of the messianic banquet; even that idea, however, is not far from the eschatological emphasis of Jewish Christianity. According to the Jewish expectations of the time, the eschatological manna would be eaten at the messianic banquet. The manna of Jewish expectations was like the eucharist, in that it pointed backward toward the past and forward to the consummation.

4 The Transfiguration

Critical Issues

As in the previous chapters, before applying Gerhardsson's method of analysis to the story of the transfiguration, we must consider the critical issues concerning this narrative. Three accounts of the transfiguration appear in the Gospels; Matthew 17:1-8, Mark 9:2-8, and Luke 9:28-36 each contain a somewhat different version of the story. Nevertheless, despite their differences, the relationship between the three accounts seems clear: Matthew and Luke have used the earlier Markan account and edited it.[1] Mark's version, then, deserves primary attention. A fourth account of the transfiguration is found in 2 Peter 1:16-18. While this version differs significantly from the accounts in the Synoptic Gospels, it seems to depend upon the stories found there,[2] and accordingly, this version is relevant only for the discussion of the theological thrust of the story.

The unity of this story is an issue still under debate. Some earlier scholars maintained that the story was composed of two originally separate pieces, one inspired by the story of the theophany on Mount Sinai (Exodus 24), and the other telling of the transfiguration proper in which Jesus was changed into a resplendent figure with "garments . . . glistening, intensely white" (Mark 9:3). However, two arguments work against such a proposal. First, there is no convincing evidence for a seam in the story where the two separate pieces were joined together. Second, the proposal assumes that each piece of the story conveys a different Christology or picture of Jesus. This assumption may owe more to the imagination of the interpreter than to adequate exegesis of the story. A more recent proposal argues not that the story consists of two originally separate pieces, but that Mark simply redacted an original pre-Markan story. Accordingly Chilton proposes that verses 7b and 8, which include the voice from the cloud and its message, were added by Mark, who found that detail in the baptismal narrative and repeated it here. On the other hand, another recent redactional treatment by G. Sellin argues that the voice was originally a part of the transfiguration story, since a voice has a genuine narrative function stemming from the Sinai tradition. Mark, Sellin continues, inserted the voice into the baptismal story from the transfiguration.[3] This is not the place to balance arguments for or against these redactional approaches, because there is no scholarly consensus on either the extent of Mark's redactional activity or the precise words of the pre-Markan tradition.

However, most critics *do* agree that as a story the narrative exhibits both unity and focus. As Kee explains, the reader's attention is skillfully pulled toward the main point of the story:

> In the text of Mark, the climax of the narrative is not in the metamorphosis of Jesus and the radiance of his clothing, but in the heavenly voice.[4]

Consequently, the following analysis treats the story as a literary unity.

Another critical issue that continues to divide scholars is the proper classification of the narrative. Some identify it as a resurrection story projected back into the ministry of Jesus; others classify it as an epiphany, and still others as an eschatological vision. Each position is noteworthy, since the form of a story points to its meaning. The proper classification bears vitally upon the following analysis of the narrative.

Robert Stein, after reviewing the most common arguments for and against the view that the transfiguration was originally a resurrection story, concludes that this view is incorrect. Perhaps the most telling argument appears in his discussion of form-critical considerations. Using C. H. Dodd as his authority, Stein shows that "in form the transfiguration contrasts with the general type of resurrection-accounts in almost every particular."[5] Clearly, the transfiguration is not a misplaced resurrection story.

In recent years the classification of the transfiguration as an epiphany story has gained wide support. If it is an epiphany, then it reveals the divine essence or godlike nature of Jesus. According to a popular expression of this view today, the words "This is my beloved Son" in Mark 9:7 designate Jesus as a "divine Man" or godlike man. This christological picture suggests that the story originated in a hellenistic or hellenistic-Jewish milieu.

In a similar manner to Stein, Kee reviews the arguments for classifying the story as an epiphany and finds that they are not exegetically sound. Those who interpret the story as an epiphany place heavy reliance upon the presence of the Greek word *metamorphoo*, which the RSV translates "he was transfigured." This interpretation, along with the glistening white garments, would indicate that the hidden divine nature of Jesus was revealed. However, this may be reading into the word a more hellenistic meaning than it was here meant to convey. Paul's use of the same word in 2 Corinthians 3:18, for example, does not support this interpretation at all:

> And we all, with unveiled face, beholding the glory of the Lord, are being changed [*metamorphoo*] into his likeness from one degree of glory to another; for this comes from the Lord who is the Spirit.

Here Paul employs the same Greek term to describe the change "we all" are now undergoing through the presence of the Holy Spirit and will continue to undergo after death. He is not describing a hidden divine nature in us. Rather, Paul's passage is to be understood within the context of apocalyptic Judaism.[6] Furthermore, as Revelation 7:13–14 makes clear, the white garments are a stock item in works that picture the end of the age. Kee concludes:

> There is no evidence, therefore, that the glistening garb of Jesus and the metamorphosis is intended to convey that he underwent a fundamental change so that his concealed divine nature became disclosed for the moment. . . . The only thing that can be inferred from the radiance is that Jesus was seen as entering proleptically into the eschatological glorification that Jewish apocalyptic expected the righteous to share in.[7]

Thus Kee exposes a fundamental misinterpretation of those who classify the transfiguration as an epiphany.

What, then, is the correct form of this story? It is possible to classify the transfiguration as a vision on the basis of a technical term and a formal characteristic that the story shares with other visions. The Greek term behind the translation "there appeared" in Mark 9:4a occurs elsewhere in descriptions of visions (Gen. 35:9; Judg. 13:3; Luke1:11; Rev. 11:19, 12:1, and 3). A formal characteristic that the transfiguration shares with other visions is the sudden fading away of Moses and Elijah in Mark 9:8. This characteristic also appears in other accounts of visions (Gen. 35:13; Judg. 6:21 and 13:20; Acts 10:7 and 10:16).[8]

Additional exegetical evidence indicates that the transfiguration should be classified as an *apocalyptic* vision, because it pictures the coming end of this age/world. In the verse immediately following the transfiguration story, Matthew 17:9, Jesus commands Peter, James, and John: "Tell no one the vision." Sabbé identifies the Greek word here translated "vision" as a technical term for an apocalyptic vision.[9] Following the parallel command in Mark 9:9 "to tell no one what they had seen," Mark adds this comment in 9:10: "So they kept the matter to themselves." The Greek word translated "matter" can be a technical expression for "vision." The same word (*logos*) is used in its technical sense of vision in a Greek version of Daniel 10:1. It is used again at the end of a vision in the LXX version of Daniel 12:8. In all these (Danielic) passages the term (*logos*) is almost the equivalent of the word "apocalypse."[10] Thus, Matthew identifies the transfiguration as an apocalyptic vision and Mark points in the same direction.

Further evidence for classifying the transfiguration as an apocalyptic vision is Kee's list of details common to Daniel 10 and Mark 9:2–8.[11] Kee cites such details as "the radiant appearance of Daniel as he receives the vision." Since Daniel 10 is an apocalyptic vision, we may infer that the transfiguration falls into the same category. Indeed, Sabbé views Daniel 10 not only as an apocalyptic vision, but also as a literary stereotype of the apocalyptic style.[12] If Daniel 10 is an apocalyptic stereotype, then the identification is even more secure.

Another justification for classifying the transfiguration as an apocalyptic vision is the exegetical traditions associated with the stories of Moses and Mount Sinai (Exod. 24 and 34:29ff). Mark 9:2–8 quotes from and is also modeled upon these passages. Furthermore, in New Testament times these Exodus stories came to be interpreted apocalyptically and became one kind of description for the coming end-of-the-world drama. Simply stated, the Moses/Sinai stories became a proper vehicle for conveying an apocalyptic vision. However, the full force of the argument can be seen only after the influence of this passage on the transfiguration has been shown and after the exegetical tradition associated with it has become clear.

My own research maintains that the story of the transfiguration is clearly an apocalyptic vision based upon the stories in Exodus 24 and 34:29ff. Accordingly, the narrative is complex and shimmering. On the one hand, it shows Jesus in eschatological glory; on the other, it deliberately recalls a central event in the wilderness wanderings of the people of Israel. But the transfiguration does not simply reflect the events on Mount Sinai. In the Jewish community the story of Mount Sinai was not static and fixed, for in its many retellings it continued to change. Like the manna, Sinai became both eschatological and apocalyptic—it came to foreshadow the end of the age.[13] Accordingly, Kee emphasizes that in the transfiguration "the eschatological end is being enacted in the conclave of Moses, Elijah, and Jesus."[14]

The climax of the story, however, lies in the words of the heavenly voice. Jesus is identified as "my beloved Son," and the voice admonishes the audience to "listen to him." Thus the story reveals the apocalyptic orientation of Jewish Christianity. Far from proclaiming a "divine Man" Christology, the heavenly voice stresses the eschatological authority of Jesus.

Details and Words from the Greek Bible

Three lines of evidence suggest that the transfiguration was modeled on Exodus 24 and Exodus 34:29ff. In the first place, a number of details, such as the six days, are common to both stories, and in both Exodus and Mark those details function similarly. The second line of evidence is the quoted word or words found within the common details, such as the Greek words for "six" and "days." Finally, the transfiguration story includes some words from the Exodus passages that have nothing to do with the common details.

An important detail occurring both in Exodus and in Mark's account of the transfiguration is the phrase "six days." Moses waited on Mount Sinai for six days (Exod. 24:16), and also "after six days" Jesus led Peter, James, and John up the mount of transfiguration (Mark 9:2). In both stories the detail plays a similar role: it precedes an encounter with God. After Moses' six-day wait, God calls to him on the seventh day; and when after six days Jesus climbs the mountain, on that seventh day the heavenly voice acknowledges him as "Son."

Other details recur as well. Both stories, for instance, have the voice of God coming out of a cloud (Exod. 24:16, Mark 9:7), and in both, the participants are covered by that cloud. The cloud indicates God's presence. Another common detail is the group of three companions. Jesus takes Peter and James and John (Mark 9:2), while Moses is commanded to bring with him Aaron, Nadab, and Abihu (Exod. 24:1). These groups also function similarly, for they see the vision but participate only as witnesses. Furthermore, Moses "alone" comes near the Lord (24:2); and after Moses and Elijah have faded away, "only" Jesus is left (9:8). "Only" is the same Greek word which is translated "alone" in the Exodus verse. The presence of the seventy elders of Israel on the mount (24:1, 9) breaks the parallelism, but the fact that on both mountains the disclosure is private recalls both the Sinai story and the apocalyptic genre.

Moses, of course, appears in both stories, but he plays two quite different roles. In Exodus Moses is the primary human actor in the presence of God, but in the transfiguration his role is that of supporting actor to both Jesus and Elijah (Mark 9:4). Another possible common detail that bears consideration is Peter's statement, "let us make three booths" (Mark 9:5), where he is apparently thinking of the temporary shelters for the feast of Succoth, mentioned in Leviticus 23:43. In Exodus 25:8 God says, "And let them make me a sanctuary" (the same Greek word means both "booth" and "sanctuary"), and in Exodus 26 and 27 God gives detailed directions for making that sanctuary. Although the differences here are apparent, there is a notable similarity in the use of the same words for "make" and "booth/sanctuary" in the mountaintop experiences.

In addition to these shared details, the two stories have several words in common. The Greek words for "six days," as we have noted, are the same. While the names of the three who accompanied Moses and Jesus obviously differ, the Greek text of Exodus 24:13 also reveals an interesting similarity in the names *Moses* and *Jesus*. The RSV reads, "So Moses rose with his servant Joshua." In Greek, however, the names *Joshua* and *Jesus* are the same, so that in the LXX Moses and Jesus (Joshua) are together on Mount Sinai. Although such a coincidence means little to a modern reader, it could mean a great deal to Jewish Christians who apparently worked with both the Greek and Hebrew texts. The Greek New Testament, incidentally, records the names *Moses* and *Jesus* as in the LXX.

The Greek words for "cloud" and for the preposition "out of" are also the same, but there is a one-word difference between the phrasing in Exodus and in Mark. Exodus 24:16 has the voice speaking out of "the midst" of the cloud; the word "midst" is lacking in Mark's prepositional phrase. Both Mark and Exodus also use the same word for "mountain," again preceded by the same preposition. Whereas Exodus 24:13 uses the article "the" (thus, "into *the* mountain"), however, Mark also inserts the adjective "high." Finally, as noted earlier, the two stories share the same Greek words for "make" and "booth/ sanctuary."

Our third category deals with words the transfiguration story has apparently quoted from the Exodus passages—words that have nothing to do with common details. While the following list is not exhaustive, it does include the most significant words. Four of the words, in fact, occur nowhere else in Mark's Gospel and thus are not words that Mark tends to use. On the other hand, they do appear in Exodus 24 or 34:29ff. These facts heighten the probability that the Jewish Christians who first formulated this story were quoting these words from the Greek text. The first such significant word, translated "appeared" in Mark 9:4, in Exodus 24:11 is translated "beheld": the chief men of the people of Israel "beheld God." The words "booths" (9:5) and "led" (9:2), though they too occur here uniquely in Mark, also appear in Exodus 24 and 25. A fourth word, "were talking," which refers to Moses and Elijah in discussion with Jesus, belongs to this list as well. It is used in Exodus 34:35 in reference to Moses' speaking with God. In Exodus 34:29–34, this root verb without the preposition occurs six times; the summary statement in verse 35—as in Mark—contains the preposition.

The word "saw," used in Mark 9:8 where the three "saw" Jesus only, appears twice in Exodus 34:30 and 35, where "the people of

Israel saw the face of Moses." It occurs again in Exodus 24:10: "they saw the God of Israel." Finally, just as the people "were afraid" (Exod. 34:30) to approach Moses, so the disciples "were exceedingly afraid" (Mark 9:6) of the sight. The LXX uses the verb, and Mark uses the cognate adjective plus a preposition for emphasis.

Below is the text of Mark 9:2–8, in which the words common to Exodus 24 and 34:29–35 are underlined, showing Mark's dependence upon the older stories. A broken line underlines the names of the three disciples, as well as Mark's cognate adjective for afraid.

(2) And after six days Jesus took with him Peter and James and John, and led them up [into] a high mountain apart by themselves; and he was transfigured before them, (3) and his garments became glistening, intensely white, as no fuller on earth could bleach them. (4) And there appeared to them Elijah with Moses; and they were talking to Jesus. (5) And Peter said to Jesus, "Master, it is well that we are here; let us make three booths, one for you and one for Moses and one for Elijah." (6) For he did not know what to say, for they were exceedingly afraid (7) And a cloud overshadowed them, and a voice came out of the cloud, "This is my beloved Son; listen to him." (8) And suddenly looking around they no longer saw any one with them but Jesus only.

Note also how a literal translation of the Septuagint of Exodus 24:15–16 looks when the words in common with Mark are underlined:

(15) And Moses went up and Joshua (Jesus) into the mountain, and the cloud hid the mountain. (16) And the glory of God came down upon Mount Sinai, and the cloud hid it six days; And the Lord called to Moses on the seventh day from the midst of the cloud. (17)

After his similar reconstruction of the transfiguration tradition, Chilton describes the relationship between Mark and Exodus 24 as follows:

At the level of tradition and redaction, it is beyond reasonable doubt that the Transfiguration is fundamentally a visionary representation of the Sinai motif of Exod. 24.[15]

The use of common details and quoted words proves that one story was modeled on the other.

Exodus 24, however, is not the only story involving Moses and

Mount Sinai that the formulators of the narrative had in mind. According to many interpreters, Jesus' transfiguration and his glistening white garments (Mark 9:2) recall the shining of Moses' face after "talking with God" (Exod. 34:29ff). Matthew and Luke make the identification with Exodus 34:29ff explicit by specifically mentioning Jesus' shining face (Matt. 17:2, Luke 9:29). On the other hand, there is precedence in Jewish apocalyptic literature for the radiance of those who come into God's presence.

Deuteronomy 18:15 is the probable source of the admonition to "listen to him" that the voice from heaven directs to the audience on the mount of transfiguration. In this verse Moses directs essentially the same words to the people concerning the Moses-like prophet whom God would raise up. The context (18:16) cites the threatening nature of God's voice from Sinai as the reason for choosing a prophet through whom God would speak.

Certainly, the apocalyptic vision in Daniel 10 influenced Matthew's version of the transfiguration story. Matthew seems to have quoted words directly from the chapter in Daniel. Since these quoted words, though, are lacking in Mark's version,[16] perhaps Matthew added these words to the Markan account which lay before him. Mark's account suggests no direct influence from Daniel 10, although that chapter could have influenced the later version as a primary example of the apocalyptic genre. Probably the Jewish Christian pre-Markan story of the transfiguration drew almost exclusively on the Sinai/Moses stories. The only exception appears to be the words "my beloved Son," which are also found in the baptismal story, Mark 1:11.

The Jewish Tradition

Since Exodus 24 and 34:29ff are the primary models for the transfiguration, the Jewish tradition of biblical interpretation associated with them can provide a crucial understanding for what they came to mean. Like other stories, the interpretation of Exodus 24 was not static; it continued to evolve in Judaism, receiving interpretations from both an eschatological and an apocalyptic perspective. The following passage from 1 Enoch 1:2-4 portrays the Sinai story in the context of the eschatological era and the final judgment:

And Enoch, the blessed and righteous man of the Lord, took up [his parable] while his eyes were open and he saw, and said, "[This is] a holy vision from the heavens which the angels showed me: and I heard from them everything and I understood. I look not for this generation but for the distant one that is coming . . . . The God of the universe, the Holy Great One, will come forth from his dwelling. And from there he will march upon Mount Sinai and appear in his camp emerging from heaven with a mighty power. And everyone shall be afraid."[17]

The Ezra apocalypse places the Sinai story in an apocalyptic context. In the seventh and last vision of that book, the revelations to Ezra and his consequent task are made parallel to the revelations on Mount Sinai and the task of Moses. However, while the revelation on Sinai is past, the revelations to Ezra concern only the future:

On the third day, . . . behold, a voice came out of a bush opposite me and said, "Ezra, Ezra." . . . Then he said to me, "I revealed myself in a bush and spoke to Moses . . . and I led him up on Mount Sinai, where I kept him with me many days; and I told him many wondrous things, and showed him the secrets of the times. . . ." Then I commanded him, saying, "These words you shall publish openly, and these you shall keep secret." And now I say to you. . . .[18]

A further example of the influence of Exodus 24 on apocalyptic literature appears in the book of Jubilees, a Palestinian book dating from approximately 100 B.C. Here the whole story takes place on Mount Sinai. Jubilees begins by quoting from Exodus 24:12 God's command to Moses to "come up to me on the mountain." God then tells an angel to *reveal* to Moses the history of creation and of the covenant people until the end.[19]

The NT, too, displays this tendency to project the Sinai theophany into the eschatological future. Revelation 4:5 relies on natural manifestations recorded in Exodus 19:16, but transfers them to the seer's vision of the throne of God. Possible additional evidence for the eschatological interpretation of Exodus 24 is a phrase from 2 Corinthians 3:18, "the glory of the Lord." That same phrase also occurs in Exodus 24:17: "Now the appearance of the glory of the LORD was like a devouring fire on the top of the mountain in the sight of the people of Israel." Of course, the primary referent in 2 Corinthians 3:18 is

Exodus 34:29ff, where the skin of Moses' face "shone" when he "came down from Mount Sinai." Nevertheless, the association of this phrase with Moses' ministry in other places makes a reference to Mount Sinai possible.[20] Regardless of which earlier text Paul had in mind, however, the passage is to be understood eschatologically and the reference to Mount Sinai is clear. In fact, the importance of Mount Sinai in some Jewish apocalyptic traditions can hardly be overstated. Just as Sinai is the place in some Jewish apocalyptic literature where the future is revealed, so in this story from Jewish Christianity, Sinai is the place that establishes the eschatological authority of Jesus.

Other elements within the transfiguration story make better exegetical sense if they, too, are interpreted from an eschatological perspective. One such element is the presence of Elijah and Moses. According to Mark 9:4, Elijah and Moses appear with Jesus. How shall we define the significance of these two figures in the scene? Elijah, like Moses, heard the voice of God on Mount Sinai, but Kee is surely correct in saying that "the evidence thus points to the conclusion that Elijah was considered in first-century Judaism as an almost exclusively eschatological figure."[21] Apparently Elijah is named first because of the strength of the eschatological expectations of the time. Also, according to Malachi 3 and 4, Elijah comes as "messenger" of "the great and terrible day of the LORD" (Mal. 4:5); thus his appearance in the transfiguration shows that the drama of the end time has arrived. Elijah's appearance, then, is entirely in keeping with an eschatological perspective for Exodus 24.

The eschatological significance of Moses is probably to be found in the words of the divine voice: "listen to him" (Mark 9:7). Most commentators hold that these words reflect Deuteronomy 18:15: "The LORD your God will raise up for you a prophet like me from among you, from your brethren—him you shall heed," because "listen to him" and "him you shall heed" translate the same Greek words. This prophet-like-Moses also figures prominently in the eschatological expectations of the Dead Sea Scrolls. Furthermore, the crowd in John 6:14 apparently reflected this expectation when they said of Jesus, "This is indeed the prophet who is to come into the world!" While the words "listen to him" are associated with a prophet-like-

Moses, however, the voice from the cloud proclaims Jesus as "my beloved Son." How can this problem be resolved?

The problem is partially addressed with a proper definition of the term "Son" in this context. I will define it more fully later on, but here I am considering the term in relation to Jewish tradition. While many interpreters want to equate "Son" with "Messiah," this equation disintegrates from two points of view. J. Jeremias maintains that the expected prophet-like-Moses is not identified with the messiah in this early period,[22] and Fitzmyer similarly rejects the equation in the light of the Jewish tradition of the time:

> [I]t would have to be established that "Son" is only intended in a messianic sense (a sense that it never has in the OT and is still to be found in Palestinian Jewish literature prior to or contemporary with the NT). Jesus is not just *Moses redivivus* or *Elias redivivus* . . . . Here the Synoptic tradition has made use of a title that is pre-Pauline and has connotations other than messiah.[23]

Defining the term "Son" in this context, most interpreters point out the relationship between this story and the story of the baptism where the words "beloved Son" also appear. Our analysis of that text showed that the divine voice was quoting not from Psalm 2:7, but from the story of the binding of Isaac in Genesis 22. Accordingly, the expression "beloved Son" refers to the Abraham/Isaac story: it is not a reference to the king, and hence should not be understood messianically.

The only remaining element in the story is Peter's suggestion, "let us make three booths, one for you and one for Moses and one for Elijah" (Mark 9:5). Apparently this, too, should be understood eschatologically. Peter's proposal about making booths relates to the eschatological understanding of the feast of booths or Succoth in NT times. As Kee has noted, late in the Hebrew Bible, the prophet Zechariah predicted that during the feast of booths Yahweh would establish his eschatological rule in Jerusalem: "Then every one that survives of all the nations that have come against Jerusalem shall go up year after year to worship the King, the LORD of hosts, and to keep the feast of booths" (Zech. 14:16).[24]

The Work of Early Jewish Christians

In discussing the early Jewish Christian background of the transfiguration story, perhaps the only thing we can note with assurance is its unity. All the elements of the narrative contribute to the whole, and the story moves steadily toward its climax—the words of the voice from the cloud, designating Jesus as the "beloved Son" and directing the hearers to "listen to him." This unity is a remarkable achievement.

However, for two reasons, it is difficult to analyze the work of the story's Jewish Christian formulators. The first is the dependence of scholarship upon the Markan account. Since Matthew and Luke derive their versions from Mark and since Second Peter depends upon the accounts in the Gospels, there is no independent witness to the pre-Markan story. In addition, the attempts of redaction critics to separate Mark's own comments from the pre-Markan narrative have not met with widespread acceptance. Only those words that occur once in Mark's Gospel and appear also in Exodus 24 give any sure indication of the pre-Markan story.

Another difficulty here is that scholars attempting to go behind the Markan account have taken widely divergent directions. Most scholars today follow one of two primary interpretations. A large number of critics, regarding this story as a conscious literary creation, assume that Jewish Christians drew on their contemporary apocalyptic traditions to produce the narrative of the transfiguration. If this proposal is correct, then the interpreter must second-guess the ancient author(s) in separating all the strands woven into such a closely-knit unity— particularly in separating the strands of traditions from the Markan redactions. This hypothesis, however, while quite congenial to modern critical scholars, disregards the apocalyptic mindset and milieu of Jewish Christianity. Visions are important, and numerous visions are recorded in the NT. Both Jesus and Paul claim to be recipients of visions; according to the book of Acts, Stephen, Peter, and others saw visions as well. Therefore, other scholars insist that the transfiguration story may be the result of an actual vision, and that the story must be explained, partially at least, in terms of the recipient's religious background and orientation.[25] This critical position makes the task of interpretation nearly impossible. Accordingly, I offer the following suggestions with some hesitation.

From a literary critical perspective, the transfiguration is based on the stories recorded in Exodus 24, Exodus 34:29ff, and other stories associated with Moses and Mount Sinai. Apparently the two primary stories concerning Mount Sinai, understood from an eschatological perspective, were the primary magnet that attracted other elements into the narrative. The theophany on Mount Sinai mentions both the voice from the cloud and the repeated commands to build the wilderness sanctuary. The Sinai voice probably attracted, as a new narrative element, the words concerning the beloved Son and prophet-like-Moses, and the commands concerning the sanctuary likely attracted the eschatological understanding of the feast of booths. Elijah, associated with Mount Sinai in his flight from Jezebel (1 Kings 19), was presumably added on the strength of the expectations in contemporary Judaism. The strong commitment of Jewish Christians to the parallelism between the generation under Moses and the time of salvation under Jesus would account for the magnetic attraction exerted by the eschatological understanding of these Sinai stories.

With considerably more assurance, I turn to the meaning of the words "beloved Son." Fitzmyer has commented (see note 23, above) that the title "Son" "is pre-Pauline and has connotations other than messiah." By "pre-Pauline" Fitzmyer apparently refers to an understanding of Jesus akin to that in the Synoptic Gospels where his entry (incarnation) into the human condition from a pre-existent state is not taught. Paul mentions both pre-existence and incarnation in various creedal statements about Jesus. Actually, Fitzmyer's description of "Son" as a "pre-Pauline" term lacking messianic "connotations" is very close to our analysis of the words "beloved Son" in the baptismal account. As Howard Marshall argues, the adjective "beloved" is an inappropriate designation for the messiah, indicating instead "the unique relationship of Jesus to his Father."

Additional light may be shed on the words "beloved Son" in the transfiguration scene by the context and origin of those same words in the baptismal narrative. Let us first review our findings concerning the origin of the words—not in Psalm 2:7 but in Genesis 22. The parallelism or typology between Jesus and Isaac enabled the early Jewish Christians to express their faith in categories with which they were familiar. As Isaac was the unique/beloved son of Abraham, so Jesus is the unique/beloved "Son" of God. This typology expressed Jesus' relationship to God without referring to categories like pre-existence and incarnation.

Furthermore, in the baptismal scene the context of the words "beloved Son" reflects the sacrificial connotations associated with the binding of Isaac. The transfiguration scene, on the other hand, comes from an eschatological and apocalyptic context that seems to emphasize the unique relationship associated with the words "beloved Son" rather than its sacrificial implications.

For Jewish Christians the words "beloved Son" possibly recalled the expressions Jesus himself used in describing his relationship to God. Vermes, who sees Jesus as one of the charismatic, holy men of Galilee, summarizes what meaning the term *son of God* would convey to early Jewish Christians:

> If the reasoning followed in these pages is correct, the earliest use of *son of God* in relation to Jesus derives from his activities as a miracle-worker and exorcist, and from his own consciousness of an immediate and intimate contact with the heavenly Father.[26]

If Jewish Christians did not recollect and transmit such remembrances of Jesus in the period after the crucifixion, who else might have done it?

Another problem of analysis lies in the juxtaposition of the words "beloved Son" with the admonition "listen to him." The command "listen to him" is associated with the prophet-like-Moses. Although the prophet was to speak God's "words" to the people, in this vision the beloved Son has become, to quote Kee, "God's spokesman for the end time."[27] Thus the function of the eschatological prophet-like-Moses has been shifted to the Son, and only the words "listen to him" are left to remind the reader of the prophet.

This shift, coupled with the subordination of Moses to the "Son" in the transfiguration scene, may reflect a theological perspective of early Jewish Christianity. Two other NT passages imply this same perspective. In the Pauline passage, 2 Corinthians 3:7–14, Jesus is presented not as a new Moses but as one who is *more* than Moses. Similarly, in the letter to the Hebrews 3:1–6, Jesus is greater than Moses just as a "son" is greater than a "servant":

> Now Moses was faithful in all God's house as a servant, to testify to the things that were to be spoken later, but Christ was faithful over God's house as a son. (Heb. 3:5–6a)

Then in the next two verses we find an OT quotation containing the same emphasis on hearing him, just like that in the transfiguration (both use the same Greek words). It also contains the now-familiar association with the wilderness generation: "Today, when you hear his voice, do not harden your hearts as in the rebellion, on the day of testing in the wilderness" (Heb. 3:7).

The precise meaning of this apocalyptic vision for the early Jewish Christians still needs clarification. In its long history of interpretation, this passage has inspired a number of views. Most of these views appear either to read meanings into the words of the text or to do violence to the text by rearranging it. Only two critical opinions—one modern, proposed by Kee, and the other traditional—seek to interpret the actual words and figures found in the story.

Earlier I quoted Kee's statement that "the eschatological end is being enacted in the conclave of Elijah, Moses, and Jesus" (see note 14, above). Kee clarifies the role of Jesus in that "eschatological end" by commenting on his radiance:

> The only thing that can be inferred from the radiance is that Jesus was seen as entering proleptically into the eschatological glorification that Jewish apocalyptic expected the righteous to share in.

In his discussion of the phrase "listen to him" in *Community of the New Age*, Kee also writes: "The Son of God, in this proleptic vision of Jesus' eschatological vindication, is God's spokesman for the end time."[28] According to Kee, then, Jesus has entered into "the eschatological glorification" in which the righteous dead share. As the transfiguration enacts that glorification, Jesus—not Moses and not Elijah—is designated as God's chosen representative.[29]

The other significant view of the transfiguration, first advanced in ancient times, interprets this story as a preview of Jesus' second coming to earth. In fact, the transfiguration was sometimes considered a prophecy of the second coming, as the NT book of Second Peter shows.[30] Modern interpreters have argued that Jesus' transfigured glory presages the glory he will have when he returns to install God's kingdom in all its fullness.

Which of these two interpretations do the words of the transfiguration support? While the two views are not so far apart as are the interpretations of the form critics, it is unlikely that the transfiguration, given its literary unity, depicts two different scenes from the eschatological drama.

The argument from Second Peter merits little serious attention in arriving at the meaning of the transfiguration. Indeed, it is easy to understand why in Second Peter the transfiguration scene argues for the certainty of the second coming. The picture of Jesus' eschatological authority as spokesman in Mark 9:2–8 does lend support to other roles he was expected to play in the coming of God's kingdom. However, while Second Peter's argument may be sound, it does not convincingly establish that the transfiguration portrays the second coming of Jesus.

The narrative of the transfiguration itself yields two indications that the story does not represent Jesus' return. The first of these is the absence of words and phrases that other NT passages associate with the parousia. In Mark 8:38, words and phrases such as "Son of man," "with the holy angels," and "comes in the glory" clearly establish that kind of association, but such phrases appear nowhere in this story. Furthermore, the words of the story simply do not depict the second coming. The transfiguration narrative culminates in the words from heaven, which confirm Kee's interpretation. Nor does the radiance of Jesus' clothing necessarily indicate a second coming, as we have seen. Accordingly, the transfiguration story itself supports the interpretation advanced by Kee and others.

The Theological Significance of the Story

We have established that the Jewish Christians focused on the role and significance of Jesus for their faith; hence the primary thrust of this narrative is christological. The Christology, however, is wrapped in such a thoroughly apocalyptic "package" that its eschatological orientation particularly stands out. Like the previous story of the manna, this narrative also conveys something of the life situation of Jewish Christianity. Therefore we must consider the eschatological packaging of the story, its picture of Jesus, and the circumstances of the community that treasured it.

The eschatological orientation of this narrative is of course presupposed by the typological parallels through which Jewish Christianity expressed theology. Again, most parallels refer to the generation under Moses; the deliverance from Egypt and the wilderness wanderings, for example, foreshadow the coming deliverance of the end times. Thus the time of Jesus and his immediate followers is the time of eschatological fulfillment and salvation.

Like previous stories we have examined, this narrative reflects a characteristic theological method and view of history. Here the basic parallel involves stories concerning Mount Sinai, which typically foreshadow the coming deliverance. Yet there is a difference. The transfiguration story heightens the eschatological tension by depicting the very end itself. Even the form of the story indicates this dramatic eschatological heightening. In the apocalyptic vision, the glistening garb of Jesus signifies his entry into the glorification reserved for the righteous, and the words from the cloud proclaim Jesus as "God's spokesman for the end time." Whereas previous stories addressed Jewish Christians in their present lives, this story pointed the people to their future destiny as well.

The transfiguration story also presents a well-focused picture of Jesus and his relationship to God. The words "beloved Son" do not define a messianic title: no messiah was ever pictured like this. "Beloved Son" does not indicate an incarnation from a pre-existent state, nor does it imply any "divine Man" concept. Rather, this phrase suggests another parallel or type explored earlier in the baptismal scene—the Isaac/Jesus typology. As Isaac was a unique/beloved son of Abraham, so here Jesus' relationship to God is that of a unique "beloved Son."

To Jewish Christian ears the words "beloved Son" possibly recalled Jesus' prayer life and miracles as well as his consciousness of an intimate and unique relationship to God. In the transfiguration scene the relationship between Father and Son includes the role assigned to Jesus as "spokesman for the end time." Peter, James, John, and the wider audience of hearers are all admonished to respond to this role and "listen to him."

The word "listen" (better translated as "hear") implies more than casual attention to chitchat, for it means "hear" in the sense of *obey* and *do*. Thus the divine admonition denotes eschatological authority. Note how this eschatological authority assigned to the "Son" in the transfiguration story agrees with the eschatological authority given to Jesus' words in the famous picture of the parousia portrayed in Mark 8:38. In both passages, hearing the words of Jesus is a central emphasis:

> For whoever is ashamed of me and of my words in this adulterous and sinful generation, of him will the Son of man also be ashamed, when he comes in the glory of his Father with the holy angels.

Consequently, the "beloved Son" is a leading character in the eschatological drama.

Another early Jewish Christian illustration of the eschatological authority of the Son appears in Matthew 7:21–23, as pointed out by H. D. Betz.[31] In this passage Jesus says:

> Not every one who says to me, 'Lord, Lord,' shall enter the kingdom of heaven, but he who does the will of my Father who is in heaven. (22) On that day many will say to me, 'Lord, Lord did we not prophesy in your name, and cast out demons in your name, and do many mighty works in your name?' (23) And then will I declare to them, 'I never knew you; depart from me, you evildoers.'

Accordingly, Jesus testifies on behalf of his followers in the last judgment. While the transfiguration emphasizes the authority of Jesus, the image of Jesus as advocate adds clarity to that authority in two ways. First, it underscores the preoccupation of early Jewish Christianity with the eschatological drama, and second, it shows that for Jewish Christians, that drama was composed of several scenes, only one of which is presented in the transfiguration.

The transfiguration also tells us something about life within the

Jewish Christian community. Such a story contributes to the self-understanding of these Jewish Christians as an eschatological community-in-waiting. They were not only living in the eschatological time of salvation inaugurated by Jesus, they were also anticipating the very consummation of that period as pictured for them in the transfiguration.

We can speculate how such a community interpreted the words "listen to him." These words of eschatological authority presumably meant both reassurance and warning. Jewish Christians were always a minority within the larger Jewish community, and sometimes they were even persecuted (1 Thess. 2:14). If recent studies are valid, with the approach of the Jewish-Roman war of A.D. 66–70 they felt pressured by the larger community to prove their loyalty as Jews. Such a minority community had very real problems—isolation, persecution, increasing pressure to support the national cause. The words "listen to him" conveyed warning against apostasy and also reassurance in the face of present adversity. As an eschatological community, the Jewish Christians anticipated the final deliverance promised to them in the transfiguration.

Perhaps the words "listen to him" also evoked a kind of spirituality associated with visions. Certainly, visions were a part of the spirituality of those Jewish Christians who wrote and read the Revelation to John. According to Acts, Peter began to preach to Gentiles because of a vision, and in Acts 11:5ff Peter explains his conduct on the basis of the vision he received. Possibly visions were one means by which Jewish Christians "listened" to the risen Christ.

In conclusion, the story of the transfiguration fits well into the overall eschatological outlook of Mark's Gospel. Both this apocalyptic vision and the little apocalypse in chapter 13 uncover the future for the reader. Also, the transfiguration performs in this Gospel a specific function. Kee elaborates:

> The one architectural feature that stands out Mark has placed at the centre of his gospel (Mark 9:2ff.), the eschatological vision of Jesus' exaltation.[32]

This "architectural feature"—the transfiguration—is preceded by the identification of Jesus as Messiah in 8:29, which identification is balanced by Jesus' statement of the necessity of his suffering and death as his role in relation to the coming of the kingdom. Thus messiahship, suffering and death, plus the eschatological vision of Jesus' exaltation, constitute the "literary fulcrum" at the center of Mark's Gospel.

5 Conclusion

In order to place the results of the foregoing research in their proper context, the following paragraphs will direct attention to the unique aspects of this study.

Unique Aspects of the Foregoing Study

Two recent books have concentrated on different literary forms employed by early Jewish Christians. H. D. Betz has studied the Jewish Christian source lying behind our present Sermon on the Mount: he classifies it as a compilation of the sayings of Jesus. Of course, these sayings deal with ethical behavior, especially as it relates to the observance of legal material in the Torah. By no stretch of the imagination can the narratives analyzed in the preceding four chapters be classified as compilations of the ethical sayings of Jesus, although the injunction to "listen to him" (Mark 9:7), found in the narrative of the transfiguration, may include Jesus' ethical teachings within its purview. Similarly, Donald Juel's *Messianic Exegesis: Christological Interpretation of the Old Testament in Early Christianity* examines OT passages, such as certain psalms, that explicate the confession of Jesus as Messiah-King. The present study, in contrast to the work of both Betz and Juel,[1] deals primarily with narratives based on the Exodus/Sinai/Wilderness cycle of stories.

Further, past scholars have studied only *individual* NT narratives, pointing out their possible Jewish Christian origins. In contrast to past studies, this book has analyzed four narratives and has addressed their theological significance both individually and as a group.

In the past, attempts to study these particular narratives have been plagued by the lack of a consistent technique of examination, as well as by the inability of the form critics to classify their "form." Gerhardsson's method of analysis has met both these needs. However, while Gerhardsson himself seems to have applied his method only to the narrative of the temptation, this study systematically and consistently examines four narratives.

Although I have followed Gerhardsson's method in the four previous chapters, that application does not guarantee that other scholars will reach the same conclusions. While "Jewish tradition" is a constituent element in each of these Jewish Christian stories, that term describes a vast category of material. Moreover, there are no guidelines for matching a given narrative with the relevant exegetical traditions that lie behind that narrative. Thus Gerhardsson himself never saw the connection between the story of the temptation and the rebuke tradition associated with Deuteronomy 1:1. Also unique to this study is the comparison between the narrative of the baptism and the exegetical traditions associated with the binding of Isaac that were later incorporated into the targums.

Gerhardsson rightly saw that words from the Torah were integral to the story of the temptation, but his analysis considered only explicit quotations from the OT. The present study refines Gerhardsson's method to include not only direct quotations, but also individual words and phrases from the Septuagint that recur in the NT narrative. Key words from Genesis 22 (in addition to the words "beloved Son"), for example, appear in Mark's account of the baptism, and many words from Exodus 16 recur in Mark's account of the feeding of the five thousand. This insight helps reveal the typological relationship between the OT and the NT narratives.

Additionally, the foregoing analysis of four narratives makes unprecedented observations about the theological reflections of those early Jewish Christians who formulated them. In simple summary, these Jewish Christians used the Exodus/Sinai/Wilderness motif to express the significance of Jesus for their faith; and the title "Son of God"/"beloved Son" is the key title through which they expressed the relationship between Jesus and God. These two examples are perhaps the leading theological motifs with which the Jewish Christians worked.

Also unique is my attempt to delineate the self-understanding of the early Jewish Christians who first formulated these stories. Analyzing and comparing four narratives enabled us to arrive at these insights.

The fact that this study considers only four narratives indicates opportunity for further study. Presumably, the Gospels contain additional Jewish Christian narratives. Perhaps the most likely candidate for future analysis is the narrative of Jesus' walking on the water, independent versions of which are found in both Mark and John. Also, in both these Gospels the narrative follows the feeding of the five thousand; this juxtaposition argues that it, too, like the feeding narrative, was a story that circulated before the Gospels were written. Also, like the other narratives considered here, it appears to be modeled on an OT story. The present study, preliminary rather than final, opens the door to additional research on the narratives formulated by early Jewish Christians.

Having pointed out the unique aspects of this study, we can best summarize the results of our research under three headings. They are the Exodus/Sinai/Wilderness motif and its wider implications, the centrality of Christology, and the self-understanding of the Jewish Christian community that formulated these four stories.

The Exodus/Sinai/Wilderness Motif

The story of the temptation in the wilderness shows that Jesus remained faithful to God in the very temptations which Israel of old had failed. It compares the wilderness generation to Jesus and draws a secondary typology between Moses and Jesus, for both are taken to a high mountain.

In the feeding of the five thousand, the typology with the wilderness generation is again clear. As God fed manna to the hungry people under the ministry of Moses, so under the ministry of Jesus hungry people are fed with the new manna. The manna was "spiritualized" in Jewish tradition in accordance with Deuteronomy 8:3;

accordingly, Jesus "feeds" the people by teaching them. In John's account of the feeding, the crowds hail Jesus as "the prophet who is to come into the world" (John 6:14), presumably in fulfillment of Moses' promise in Deuteronomy 18:15ff that God would raise up a prophet like him.

The primary stories lying behind the transfiguration account are found in Exodus 24 and Exodus 34:29ff, and a supplementary allusion comes from Deuteronomy 18:15. Jewish tradition interpreted the theophany on Mount Sinai from an eschatological perspective so that the final deliverance, in which Jesus is pictured in eschatological glory, is again patterned after the first deliverance under Moses.

The story of the baptism hints at the typology with the deliverance at the sea, but does not develop it. As Israel went through the sea and then wandered in the wilderness, so Jesus is baptized in the river and then is led into the wilderness.

The emphasis on the Exodus/Sinai/Wilderness story in early Jewish Christianity is the expression of the theology of history common to many Jews of the time. This way of viewing history begins with the Exodus itself. For a long time scholars recognized that the Exodus story provided the central pattern of deliverance in the Hebrew Bible.[2] In Second Isaiah the first Exodus became the guarantee of a new exodus from Babylonian captivity. When the return from Babylon proved to be a disappointment, the hope for a new exodus continued to excite the expectations of the people.

This hope continued to be a prominent motif in Judaism, especially in the Dead Sea Scrolls community, which patterned its life after the first wilderness generation under Moses. In addition to the Qumran community, Josephus mentions a series of "messianic" figures, such as Theudas, who led their followers into the wilderness to reenact a new redemption patterned on the first.

In view of this widespread expectation of a new deliverance modeled after the old, it is not surprising that early Jewish Christians explained their faith in Jesus in terms of parallels or types drawn from the generation under Moses. Indeed, Paul shows his knowledge of the same motif in such passages as 1 Corinthians 10:1–13 and 2 Corinthians 3:7–18. This theology of history has been stated concisely by

Bertil Gärtner: "The salvation of the people out of Egypt is the pattern for the coming salvation."[3]

Note how these stories explain the "coming salvation" in Jesus. The story of the temptation shows how Jesus prompts the age of salvation by remaining faithful to God: breaking the power of Satan, he thereby inaugurates the coming deliverance. Here Jesus is binding the strong man and plundering his kingdom. The five thousand sons of Israel eating manna also herald the age to come. Furthermore, just as in Jewish apocalyptic literature Mount Sinai was the place where God revealed the future, so in the transfiguration that same mountain is the place where God presents the eschatological authority of Jesus.

While Gärtner's statement is correct, it does not contain the whole truth that our limited analysis has unveiled. These early Jewish Christians' list of types included other redemptive events which also served as a "pattern for the coming salvation." Such an event was the binding of Isaac. A kind of prototypical sacrifice which validated all future sacrifices on the temple mount, it foreshadowed the sacrifice of Jesus which insured the forgiveness of sin. In addition to the Exodus/Sinai/Wilderness motif, then, other redemptive events from the Hebrew Bible point to the salvation inaugurated by Jesus. Consequently this view of history—which assumes that the themes of past generations will repeat grandly at the end of the age—is the theological presupposition implicit in each narrative analyzed here.

However, expressing theology by drawing parallels with Israel's past implies more than announcing the presence of the coming salvation in Jesus. This theological method is thoroughly apocalyptic, for it presupposes a doctrine of two ages: this present evil age is being superseded by God's coming good age. Although the present evil time is under the rule of Satan, through Christ's deliverance God's rule has begun. The new age is dawning, Satan is being defeated, sin has been forgiven on the cross, and salvation is at hand.

Yet there is a subtle difference here from most other apocalyptic schemes, in which the transition from this age to the age to come is sharp and sudden. Here, the two ages overlap. Satan has been defeated, but he has not yet lost the war. The eschatological manna has been eaten, but the messianic banquet is still to come. In a *vision* the

Son has appeared in eschatological glory, but in the *world* the battle against sin, death, and the devil still rages. Although the Jewish Christians have witnessed the dawning of the new age, they still await full salvation.

Christology

Also related to the emphasis on the Exodus/Sinai/Wilderness motif is early Jewish Christians' preoccupation with Christology, or the significance of Jesus.

In the story of the temptation in the wilderness, Jesus succeeds where Israel failed. Remaining obedient to God, Jesus breaks Satan's power over the creation, inaugurates the age of deliverance, and demonstrates his Sonship. This strong, clear image of Christ becomes somewhat muted in the NT accounts of the feeding of the five thousand. Although in John 6:14f the crowds respond to the feeding by hailing Jesus as "the prophet who is to come" and by attempting to "make him king," neither Mark nor John develops these christological titles. Rather, they emphasize Jesus' teaching in the context of the feeding. This teaching seems to reflect the spiritualized understanding of manna whereby manna is equated with moral and religious instruction.

In the transfiguration a voice again identifies Jesus as a "beloved Son." While the "Son" is pictured in eschatological glory, special significance is attached to his words or teaching, for the audience is instructed to "listen to him." Thus the story points to Jesus' eschatological authority. The words "beloved Son," quoted from Genesis 22, also appear in Mark 1:11. As Isaac was the unique/beloved son of Abraham, so Jesus is the unique/beloved "Son" of God. This typological mode of thinking enabled Jewish Christians to express their faith in familiar terms—and, significantly, it does not refer to the messiah.

The above survey of four passages, though narrow, reveals several important insights that early Jewish Christians held. First, it illustrates the richness and depth of their christological thinking. They were not content to limit their notions of Jesus to some simple category like "messiah," as the later Jewish Christian Ebionites tended to do. They did not confine Jesus' role to "one 'episode in salvation history' among others"[4]; rather, they linked God's past revelation to Israel with the present eschatological deliverance of Jesus. Nor did they confine their search for types to the Exodus/Sinai/Wilderness generation alone; they drew parallels between Jesus and Isaac as well.

The above survey also suggests that the early Jewish Christians' primary definition of Jesus' significance was Sonship. Jesus is called "beloved Son" and "Son of God" in three of the four passages cited above. While this conclusion is true for our limited survey, however, it may not be true for early Jewish Christianity as a whole, since this study covers only narratives and does not include christological titles.

Nevertheless, the crucial point is the meaning of the term "Son" as used by Jewish Christians. This title, understood as nonmessianic and nonincarnational, emphasized an intimate relationship to God. The concept of the messiah and later developments such as pre-existence must not be read into it. The Abraham/Isaac story partially defines that intimate/unique relationship, but Sonship also receives definition through what Jesus *does*, since each of the passages points to a significant activity of Jesus. Jesus' obedience in defiance of Satan's power demonstrates his Sonship; the death of the Son opens a new channel of forgiveness for the redeemed community; and the picture of the Son in eschatological glory, along with the words "listen to him," emphasizes his authority in the period of deliverance.

Further, for Jewish Christians, the term "Son of God" possibly carried recollections of the ministry and prayer life of Jesus. Vermes, in fact, traces the title back to Jesus himself and discovers its meaning in contemporary Judaism. These findings support the suggestion of Martin Hengel that the title "Son of God" was the contribution of Jewish Christianity to the church.[5]

The Self-understanding of Early Jewish Christians

The analyses of the four NT stories reveal elements of the self-understanding of the Jewish Christian community. One such element is the image of an eschatological community-in-waiting. Since the theology of history implicit in every one of the four NT stories indicates that the age of fulfillment has dawned, the Jewish

Christians who formulated these stories understandably regarded themselves as an eschatological community. Indeed, this self-understanding is nowhere clearer than in the feeding of the five thousand, where the repetition of the manna miracle in the ministry of Jesus signifies that the eschatological age has arrived. Also significant is the use of eucharistic formulas to describe the feeding miracle. Jewish Christians were fed by the eschatological sacrament both in recognizing that they were living during the time of salvation and were remembering the giving of the manna under Moses and the new manna under Jesus.

However, the transfiguration, which pictured Jesus in eschatological glory, added a peculiar intensity to their waiting. They were uniquely situated between the times: while the age of fulfillment had begun, the very end of this present evil age and the beginning of the new age to come had been pictured. These Jewish Christians were experiencing the last stages of the present age. The publication of Luke's and John's Gospels, which addressed the problematic delay of the full coming, was still in the distant future, and so the people's hopes were apparently very intense. In addition, the gathering clouds of the great Jewish war against Rome must have fanned hopes that the end of this present evil age was fast approaching.

Related to this self-understanding was a form of spirituality which centered on visions, even as today the spirituality of some focuses on speaking in tongues. The frequency of visions in apocalyptic literature in general and in the NT in particular accentuates this characteristic. According to Acts, Peter made a basic decision on the basis of a vision. Visions were also one way people could "listen" to the risen and exalted Lord.

The Jewish Christians furthermore understood themselves as a "school" or scholarly community, much like the school that flourished at Qumran at the same time, possibly not many miles away. In both cases, the school was supported and sustained by a larger community. All members of the larger community were not members of the school, but they all shared its literary output. While it may be a coincidence that the school at Qumran and the Jewish Christian school shared a similar apocalyptic outlook, it is more likely that the two schools expressed and also resulted from that outlook. Both schools shared the belief that the Mosaic age foreshadowed the coming age of salvation, and both searched the Scriptures to show how the ancient texts were being fulfilled in the present.

An examination of these four Jewish Christian narratives provides strong evidence that they were the product of a scholarly community or school. The balance and parallelism of the temptation story reveal a sophistication shared by all four stories, seen also in the midrash-like interaction between the words from Torah and the first-century stories about Jesus. These stories again call to life the words from Torah, while the words from Torah explain and clarify the stories. While the words from Torah furnish the context, the life of Jesus reenacts the ancient narratives.

The members of the "school" also knew the exegetical traditions associated with the Hebrew Bible and unobtrusively allowed these traditions to constitute the background of the stories they formulated. For example, the rebuke tradition associated with Deuteronomy 1:1 dictated that the three passages quoted by Jesus should be taken from that book. Exegetical traditions associated with Genesis 22, constituting the background of the story of the baptism, seem to dictate the literary form of Mark's account—which is later found in written form in the targums. Similar traditions concerning the eschatological manna and the eschatological importance of Sinai also make intelligible the feeding of the five thousand and the transfiguration.

Like the Qumran school, the Jewish Christian community could work in several languages. My research suggests that the rebuke tradition was known in both the Hebrew Damascus Document and the Hebrew Jubilees. The relevant exegetical traditions concerning Isaac were also known in Aramaic. Yet the school also worked in Greek, using the Septuagint as they skillfully wove words from that source into the fabric of their narratives.

To drive home the point here, some group worked in several languages; some group knew the exegetical traditions associated with words from Torah; and some group formed a midrash-like interaction between the words from Torah and the stories about Jesus. Furthermore, some group wrote the stories to exhibit a remarkable unity and theological purpose. All these achievements add up to a tremendous burst of intellectual energy, and as at Qumran, they indicate the existence of a school or scholarly community.

The literary products of Jewish Christianity clearly bear the marks of an ancient "school," but those products were designed for practical ends like apologetics and evangelism. In formulating the stories, this "school" exploited the hopes and aspirations of the contemporary Jewish community. We have seen that both the Dead Sea Scrolls and Josephus witness to the strength of the Exodus/Sinai/Wilderness motif in contemporary Judaism. Three of the four stories we have analyzed are modeled on biblical stories associated with that motif, and they picture Jesus as the motif's fulfillment. Certainly, the theme of promise and fulfillment was a reassuring apologetic (defense of the faith) for members of the Jewish Christian community, as the later Gospels of Matthew and John also found it to be. At the same time, in view of the intense eschatological expectations of the period, the message of the fulfillment of the Exodus/Sinai/Wilderness motif in Jesus would exert a powerful attraction on Jews outside the community.

The growing veneration for Moses in contemporary Judaism[6] seems to have posed a real challenge for Jewish Christian apologetics. On the one hand, Moses was associated with the prophet to come (Deut. 18:15), while on the other hand, a primary christological category of Jewish Christianity was "Son." Note how in two places the Jewish Christians blended the Jewish veneration for Moses and the expectation of a Moses-like prophet into the "Son" figure. In the story of the temptation in the wilderness, the secondary parallel with Moses on Mount Nebo in the third temptation is applied to the "Son," and the words "listen to him" (which Moses originally spoke of the coming prophet) are now spoken by the voice from the cloud concerning Jesus. Also, the shining skin of Moses' face is "fulfilled" in the radiance of Jesus' whole being at the transfiguration. The traditional Jewish eschatological expectations concerning Moses are thus directed to the "Son."

Beyond the Evidence

The possible existence of such a school and eschatological community-in-waiting raises additional questions and shows the need for further research. This study has focused on narratives whose dominant Christology is expressed by the terms "Son of God" and "beloved Son." In one narrative the Sonship of Jesus was demonstrated by obedience, and that theme runs through other narratives as well. The voice from heaven calls for obedience to the words of Jesus; in the baptismal narrative the obedience of Isaac, to both Abraham and God, lies in the background. This obedient, nonmessianic Son of God Christology is a stark contrast to the Messiah-King Christology of Juel's research. Why did the narratives emphasize one kind of Christology and the genre investigated by Juel focus on another? Is one earlier than the other? Are we talking about the same Jewish Christians or about two different groups? Were they situated in different geographical areas? Is this the old dichotomy between Mount Sinai and Mount Zion? Are we dealing with a Galilean community that revered obedience and eschewed power, as opposed to a Jerusalem community that emphasized messiahship? Not only is further research needed, but also scholars who specialize in the social setting of early Christianity need to bring their expertise to bear on these questions.

The christological achievements of such a Jewish Christian "school" address an issue raised by Hengel in his book *The Son of God*. Discussing the development of Christology, he describes the "first two decades" after the crucifixion/resurrection as a "primal event":

> [M]ore happened in this period of less than two decades than in the whole of the next seven centuries, up to the time when the doctrine of the early church was completed.[7]

While our study of early Jewish Christianity encompasses approximately double that period, the Christology contained in the four stories analyzed above does much to explain the Jewish Christian contribution to the development of Christology during that "primal event."

This study also raises a further question: are scholars now able to speak of a Son of God trajectory stretching from early Jewish Christianity (and possibly Jesus himself) to the "high" Christology of the Gospel of John? The meaning of the title, summarized earlier, finds further development in the Gospel of Matthew. Matthew incorporates all four of the narratives that we have analyzed and adds additional "freight" to the meaning of the title "Son of God." According to this Gospel, Jesus is conceived by the Holy Spirit, since Mary is a virgin. Further, the true significance of the virgin's Son is given in the name "Emmanuel (which means, God with us)" (Matt. 1:23). Thus God is in some sense present through Jesus. Matthew stands between the early Jewish Christian understanding of this title and its highly developed Johannine meaning. John attributes to the Son pre-existence with God, portraying him as the agent of creation who is also "one" with God.

Strikingly, this trajectory or development in the meaning of this christological title takes place within Jewish Christian groups, although it develops over a span of years. If the Jewish Christians of this study flourished between A.D. 30 and 70, and if Matthew is dated around A.D. 85 and John sometime in the last decade of the century, a time span of seventy years is involved. During that time the title picked up more and more freight, so to speak. Since both Matthew and John were written for Jewish Christian churches, both early and later Jewish Christians continued to treasure and work with this title.

Further Implications

What, finally, is the significance of this study? Does it have any relationship to our life today? Three answers suggest themselves. First of all, this study clarifies the meaning of four crucial narratives about Jesus—narratives which have puzzled scholars, preachers, and lay people alike. These stories are strange because their background disappeared long ago; I have recreated that background to help explain what they meant to those who first heard them. We no longer have to read meanings into these narratives, for now we can ascertain exactly what they are saying about Jesus.

As a second implication, these early Christian narratives may be able to help people today in their thinking about Jesus. In a time when many are puzzled by creeds and by statements about the pre-existence of the Son, images of Jesus from these ancient stories may shed light. The narratives portray Jesus, for example, as a Son who remains obedient to God in the presence of temptations to which others have succumbed. The picture about the end of this age, framed by the narrative of the transfiguration, is particularly appealing today. Obedience to Jesus' words can help lead us through these troubled times into God's time and presence at the end of this life and age. Finding new life in Christ is like tasting God's manna from heaven.

This book also opens up a lost chapter in church history. The Jewish Christian narratives help us understand how Jewish we really are. In these stories we come to know Jesus according to the Judaism of his day. Fresh understandings, the saving significance of Jesus' death revealed in the baptismal account, can create a new opening for dialogue and fellowship with contemporary Jews.

Notes

Introduction

1. Jean Daniélou, *The Theology of Jewish Christianity*, vol. 1 of *The Development of Christian Doctrine Before the Council of Nicaea* (Chicago: Henry Regnery, 1964), 55–64.
2. Richard Longenecker, *The Christology of Early Jewish Christianity*, Studies in Biblical Theology, 2d ser., 17 (London: SCM, 1970), 3.
3. Birger Gerhardsson, *The Testing of God's Son: An Analysis of an Early Christian Midrash* (Lund, Sweden: Gleerup, 1966), 12. In the description of Gerhardsson's method I have used his categories, but twice used my own terminology. For example, I have used the phrase "Jewish tradition" because it is a term in current usage.
4. Geza Vermes, *Jesus and the World of Judaism* (Philadelphia: Fortress, 1984). See chap. 6, esp. 84f. from which the following quotations are taken.
5. Vermes, *Jesus and Judaism*, 85.
6. Leander E. Keck, "The Spirit and the Dove," *New Testament Studies* 17 (1970–71):67.

Chapter 1

1. Rudolf Bultmann, *The History of the Synoptic Tradition*, tr. John Marsh (New York: Harper & Row, 1963), 248. So also Barnabas Lindars who says the baptism "has become itself the moment of revelation" of Jesus as Messiah (*New Testament Apologetic: The Doctrinal Significance of the Old Testament Quotations* [Philadelphia: Westminster, 1961], 146).
2. Alan Richardson, *An Introduction to the Theology of the New Testament* (London: SCM, 1958), 150.
3. Richardson, 180.

4. George Foot Moore, *Judaism in the First Centuries of the Christian Era* (Cambridge: Harvard U. Press, 1932), 1: 539.

5. F. Josephus, *Jewish Antiquities*, I:232, tr. H. St. J. Thackeray (Cambridge: Harvard U. Press, 1957), 4: 115. Isaac's age is found in I:227, p. 113. In a later account Isaac is thirty-seven years old. See *Midrash Rabbah: Genesis* LV.4 (London: Soncino, 1977), 485.

6. Vermes, *Scripture and Tradition in Judaism* (Leiden: Brill, 1973), 36.

7. Richardson, 180, and Vermes, *Scripture and Tradition*, 222–23. The phrase found in Genesis 22:12 and again in 22:16 is *tou huiou sou tou agapetou*. Also see I. Howard Marshall, "Son of God or Servant of Yahweh?—A Reconsideration of Mark I.11," *NTS* 15 (1968–69): 334.

8. *Mekilta de-Rabbi Ishmael*, ed. Lauterbach, vol. 1 (Philadelphia: Jewish Publication Society, 1976), Pischa 7, 57: "*And When I See the Blood.* I see the blood of the sacrifice of Isaac. For it is said: 'And Abraham called the name of that place Adonai-jireh' (The Lord will see), etc. (Gen. 22:14)."

9. Marshall, 334. He goes on to say that the argument loses its weight if the saying is not dependent on the Septuagint. Paul G. Bretscher ("Exodus 4:22–23 and the Voice from Heaven," *Journal of Biblical Literature* 87 [1968]:301–11) also argues that the case for Psalm 2:7 is weak. Along with others he feels that in the original tradition the voice spoke in the third person.

10. Marshall, 336. See also Joseph A. Fitzmyer's discussion of the Lukan baptismal scene (*The Gospel According to Luke*, Anchor Bible, 28 [Garden City, NY: Doubleday, 1981], 485–86.) See also James D. G. Dunn, *Jesus and the Spirit* (Philadelphia: Westminster, 1975).

11. G. Schrenk, *Theological Wordbook of the New Testament* (Grand Rapids: Eerdmans, 1967), 2: 740ff. So also W. Michaelis, *TWNT*, 5:353.

12. For the targumic evidence see Fritzleo Lentzen-Deis, *Die Taufe Jesu nach den Synoptikern* (Frankfort Am Main: Knecht, 1970), 211.

13. Jubilees 17:16. See *The Old Testament Pseudepigrapha*, ed. James H. Charlesworth (Garden City, NY: Doubleday, 1985), 2:90. The *Ge'ez* that is translated as "pleased" is possibly a translation of *eudokeo*. See Augustus Dillmann, *Lexicon* (Lipsiae: 1865). Column 800 cites Sir. 37:28 for this verb representing *eudokeo*.

14. Lentzen-Deis, chap. 4 and 5, 97–248. Lentzen-Deis assigned a Palestinian *Hintergrund* to the *Deute-Vision* since it is found in the Targums. Thus he comes to much the same conclusion as Keck about the background of this narrative (see introduction, n. 6, above).

15. Lentzen-Deis, 209. So also Vermes, *Scripture and Tradition*, 195, n. 6. Outside these three Targums the content of Isaac's vision varies with the

source. Sometimes it is the angels of heaven, sometimes the Shekinah, sometimes the Holy One.

16. Ephraim E. Urbach, *The Sages: Their Concepts and Beliefs*, tr. Israel Abrahams (Jerusalem: Magnes, 1975), 43. Also see the discussion by Alan Unterman, "Shekhinah," *Encyclopaedia Judaica* (Jerusalem: Macmillan, 1971), 14:cc. 1350-54.

17. Marcus Jastrow, *A Dictionary of the Targumim, Talmud Babli Yerushalmi and Midrashic Literature* (New York: Judaica, 1985), 574. See Lentzen-Deis, 239-40.

18. Lentzen-Deis, 270.

19. *Midrash Rabbah: Song of Songs*, tr. M. Simon (London: Soncino, 1939), 86. While this midrash "was apparently redacted in Erez Israel about the middle of the sixth century C.E.," it contains "much original tannaitic and amoraic material" (Moshe David Herr, "Song of Songs Rabbah," *Encyclopaedia Judaica* 15:c.153).

20. *Midrash Rabbah: Deuteronomy*, tr. J. Rabinowitz (London: Soncino, 1977), 160. This midrash is late. This characteristic of the dove is noted in several *Midrashim*. See Shalom Spiegel, *The Last Trial* (New York: Behrman, 1979), 146, n. 39: "Note the dove—all other birds when they are slaughtered shudder; but the dove is not like that. On the contrary, it stretches forth its neck" (found in *Tanhuma*, ed. Buber, Tesawweh II: 96).

21. Spiegel, 146.

22. Dunn, *Jesus and the Spirit*, 62-67.

23. A. Marmorstein, *Studies in Jewish Theology*, ed. J. Rabinowitz and M. S. Lew (Freeport, NY: Books for Libraries, 1950), 131. Also, it should not be surprising that in Matthew and John, the Gospels written particularly for Jewish-Christian constituencies, Jesus, the bearer of the Spirit, should also be identified with the Shekinah. See J. Sievers, "'Where Two or Three . . .': The Rabbinic Concept of Shekhinah and Matthew 18:20," *Standing Before God*, ed. Asher Finkel and Lawrence Frizzell (New York: KTAV, 1981), 171-82; and Raymond Brown, *The Gospel According to John*, Anchor Bible 29 (Garden City, NY: Doubleday, 1966), 33.

24. Vincent Taylor calls the Lukan and Matthean terms "the more Jewish terms" (*The Gospel According to Mark* [London: Macmillan, 1955], 160). Bultmann notes, "The use of *to pneuma* absolutely is a decisive pointer to the conclusion that Mk 1: 9-11 could not have come from the Palestinian Church" (251). However, Martin McNamara disputes this: "We should note how Pseudo-Jonathan (like Paul in 2 Cor. 3:17) uses the term 'Spirit' not 'Holy Spirit' which was the usual Jewish expression" (*Targum*

and Testament: Aramaic Paraphrases of the Hebrew Bible: A Light on the New Testament [Grand Rapids: Eerdmans, 1972], 112).

25. McNamara, 108.
26. Kee's translation, from *The Old Testament Pseudepigrapha*, 1: 795. However, Anders Hultgård translates the passage differently ("The Idea. 'Levite,' the Davidic Messiah, and the Saviour Priest in the Testaments of the Twelve Patriarchs," in *Ideal Figures in Ancient Judaism*, ed. George W. E. Nickelsburg and John J. Collins [Chico, CA: Scholars, 1980], 100).
27. Vermes, *Scripture and Tradition*, 195.
28. Moses Mielziner, *Introduction to the Talmud* (New York: Bloch, 1968), 143. For our purposes it does not matter whether the tearing of the curtain is a sign of God's judgment on the temple or whether it is a sign that access to God is now open and visible as a result of the cross.
29. Harry L. Chronis, "The Torn Veil: Cultus and Christology in Mark 15:37–39," *JBL* 101 (1982): 114.
30. Chronis, 112.
31. Chronis, 100 and 109f.
32. Vermes, *Jesus and Judaism*, 84. Here I am following closely the argument that Vermes develops in chap. 6, "Jewish Literature and the New Testament Exegesis: Reflections on Methodology."
33. Robert Hayward, "The Present State of Research into the Targumic Account of the Sacrifice of Isaac," *Journal of Jewish Studies* 32 (Autumn 1981): 133. Hayward argues against the position of Davies and Chilton that the *Aqedah* is a substitute for the temple and its sacrifices. See P. R. Davies and B. D. Chilton, "The Aqedah: A Revised Tradition History," *Catholic Biblical Quarterly* 40 (Oct. 1978): 514–46.
34. Sam K. Williams, *Jesus' Death as Saving Event: The Background and Origin of a Concept*, Harvard Dissertations in Religion 2 (Missoula, MT Scholars, 1975), 202.

Chapter 2

1. Jacques Dupont, "L'Arrière-fond Biblique du Récit des tentations de Jésus," *NTS* 3 (1956–57): 299. So also his later monograph, *Les tentations de Jésus au désert*, Studia Neotestamentica, no. 4 (Bruges: Desclée de Brouwer, 1968).
2. Bultmann, 254 and 256.
3. Bultmann, 257.
4. Fitzmyer, 508; Taylor, 80.

5. Gerhardsson, 11. So also M. D. Goulder, *Midrash and Lection in Matthew* (London: SPCK, 1974), 245.

6. Gerhardsson, 42.

7. *Sifrei Deuteronomy*, ed. Louis Finkelstein (New York: Jewish Theological Seminary, 1969), 1, lines 1–3. The translation is mine.

8. The Community Rule 8:13–15. From *The Rule of Qumran and Its Meaning*, tr. A. R. C. Leaney (London: SCM, 1966), 209. The following quotations from The Community Rule will follow this translation.

9. Robert W. Funk, "The Wilderness" *JBL* 77 (1959): 214. If Funk is correct, the second and third temptations were also located in the wilderness. Funk seeks to determine "whether this . . . phrase was localized in proximity to the holy land and the holy mountain, Zion" (206). Hence the temple borders the wilderness. The "high mountain" echoes Moses' ascent to Nebo, located among "the eastern slopes of the valley" where the Lord "showed him all the land" (Deut. 34:1).

10. Ulrich Mauser, *Christ in the Wilderness*, Studies in Biblical Theology, no. 39 (Naperville, IL: Allenson, 1963), 147.

11. William R. Stegner, "Wilderness and Testing in the Scrolls and in Matthew 4:1–11," *Biblical Research* 12 (1967), 22–27.

12. Moshe David Herr, "Sifrei," *Encyclopaedia Judaica* 14:cc. 1519–21. This Tannaitic work was "arranged and edited in Erez Israel, but not before the end of the fourth century C.E." (c. 1519). Thus the date of much of the contents is earlier than the date of the arranging and editing of the book.

13. *Sifrei Deuteronomy*, 1–8.

14. *Neophyti 1*, vol. V *Deuteronomy*, ed. Alejandro Macho; (Madrid: 1978); *The Fragmentary Targum*, ed. Moses Ginsburger (Berlin: S. Calvary & Co., 1899); *Pseudo-Jonathan*, ed. Moses Ginsburger (Berlin: S. Calvary & Co., 1903); *Targum Onkelos*, ed. A. Berliner (Berlin: Gorzelanczyk & Co., 1884). The "translation" in Onkelos is much shorter than those in the other three targums.

15. *The Midrash Rabbah: Deuteronomy*, 2f. See also Exodus Rabbah 51:8 where this sentence occurs: "Hence did Moses rebuke them with: *and Laban, and Hazeroth, and Di-zahab.* (Deut. 1:1)." Here three different place-names from the same verse are quoted, strengthening the impression that a tradition focused on three sins. See *The Midrash Rabbah: Exodus*, vol. 3, tr. S. Lehrman (London: Soncino, 1977), 571.

16. Herbert Danby, *The Mishna* (London: Oxford U. Press, 1933), 456.

17. Judah Goldin, *The Fathers According to Rabbi Nathan*, vol. X, Yale Judaica Series (New Haven, Yale U. Press, 1955), 136–37, chap. 34.

18. It is difficult to know whether *The Fathers According to Rabbi Nathan* should be assigned to the Talmudic period or the Tannaitic. Goldin distinguished between the date of the compilation and the date of composition, and assigns the composition to the "tannaite" period. See Goldin, xxi. However, the rebuke tradition is cited in the Babylonian Talmud in Berakoth 32a to illustrate the statement: "R. Eleazar also said: Moses spoke insolently towards heaven. . . ." *The Talmud, Zera'im* 1, *Berakoth*, tr. M. Simon (London: Soncino, 1948), 195f.

19. Vermes, *The Dead Sea Scrolls in English* (Baltimore: Penguin, 1966), 99.

20. Jubilees 1:7, *The Old Testament Pseudepigrapha*, 2:52. Also, in Pseudo-Philo 12:4 there is a rebuke upon the wilderness generation although no words from Deuteronomy seem to be associated with it. See Pseudo-Philo, *LAB* 12:4, p. 320. For additional support in Josephus and other pre-mishnaic personages see Bruce Malina, *The Palestinian Manna Tradition* (Leiden: Brill, 1968), 72–74, and esp. 72, n. 2.

21. Bultmann, 256.

22. Dupont, "L'Arrière-fond," 292.

23. Peder Borgen, *Bread From Heaven*, Suppl. to Novum Testamentum, vol. 10 (Leiden: Brill, 1965). So also Malina.

24. Gerhardsson, 51. The above discussion follows Gerhardsson closely; see especially his pages 34, 26, and 25.

25. Fitzmyer, 511.

26. In the midrashic exposition of Psalm 91 the first few verses are interpreted to point to the security of the temple while the latter verses point to God's protection against the demons by means of the angels. The midrashic exposition fits the scene perfectly. Could it have been known in NT times? The midrash is late. See William G. Braude, *The Midrash on Psalms*, Yale Judaica Series 13 (New Haven, Yale U. Press, 1959), 100–107.

27. Dupont, *Les tentations de Jésus*, 20 and 96; G. H. P. Thompson, "Called—Proved—Obedient: A Study in the Baptism and Temptation Narratives of Matthew and Luke," *Journal of Theological Studies* n.s. 11 (1960): 7. So also Gerhardsson.

28. Gerhardsson, 20. So also P. Bonnard, "La signification du désert, selon le Nouveau Testament," *Hommage et reconnaissance . . . Karl Barth* (Neuchâtel: Delachaux & Niestlé, 1946), 12–13.

29. Gerhardsson, 22. Gerhardsson continues to argue, perhaps less cogently, that the title "Son of God" must also be derived from Deuteronomy. Since Deuteronomy is the source of key words and terms within the

story, the word for "son" is probably also derived from the comparison found in Deuteronomy 8:5: "Know then in your heart that, as a man disciplines his son, the LORD your God disciplines you." Gerhardsson considers this comparison similar to that in Hosea 11:1, which speaks of all Israel as God's son: "When Israel was a child, I loved him/ and out of Egypt I called my son." He points to other passages such as Deuteronomy 1:31; 14:1; and 32:5, 6, and 18–20. I am arguing that "Son of God" is best defined by the baptismal story in view of the close connection between the two stories. Gerhardsson seems to overlook the importance of context. Nevertheless, certainty is not possible in a case like this.

30. Richardson, 150. Richardson follows numerous others in citing this parallel relationship.
31. Marshall, 336.
32. Dupont, "L'Arrière-fond," 304.
33. Gerhardsson, 77. Gerhardsson argues that in this test Jesus is ready to love God "even if God takes his soul." See 71–83 for his full development of this theme. As Dupont says, "the argument appears to be fragile" (*Les tentations*, 22, n. 24). Certainly, the argument involves some "psychologizing" in its behalf.

Chapter 3

1. Brown, 244.
2. Taylor, 630f; Bultmann, 217. The "function" that each story performs in Mark's Gospel will be discussed later.
3. Karl Paul Donfried, "The Feeding Narratives and the Marcan Community: Mark 6, 30–45, and 8, 1–10," in *Kirche: Festschrift für Günther Bornkamm zum 75. Geburtstag*, ed. D. Lührmann and Georg Strecker (Tübingen: J. C. B. Mohr, 1980), 95–96.
4. Bultmann, 217.
5. Martin Dibelius, *From Tradition to Gospel* (New York: Charles Scribner's Sons, n.d.), 95.
6. Paul J. Achtemeier, "The Origin and Function of the Pre-Marcan Miracle Catenae," *JBL* 91 (1972): 205f.
7. Fitzmyer, 764. Unfortunately, none of the above critics, including Fitzmyer, takes into account the midrashic character of the narrative.
8. Ernst Bammel, "The Feeding of the Multitude," in *Jesus and the Politics of His Day*, ed. Ernst Bammel and C. F. D. Moule (Cambridge: Cambridge U. Press, 1984), 217.

9. Howard Clark Kee, *Community of the New Age: Studies in Mark's Gospel* (Philadelphia: Westminster, 1977), 111. The situation here is similar to that in chapter 1 where the baptism is modeled on the binding of Isaac.

10. Quentin Quesnell, *The Mind of Mark: Interpretation and Method through the Exegesis of Mark 6, 52* (Rome: Pontifical Biblical Institute, 1969), 231.

11. Mauser; see pages 134–37 where Mauser lists other examples.

12. Kee, *Community of the New Age*, 111.

13. Austin Farrer, *A Study in St. Mark* (New York: Oxford U. Press, 1952), 291.

14. Farrer, 291.

15. Achtemeier, 220f.

16. W. D. Davies, *The Setting of the Sermon on the Mount* (Cambridge: Cambridge U. Press, 1964), 49. Davies is commenting on Matthew, but Matthew copied the detail from Mark. Second Baruch 29:4 mentions Leviathan as "nourishment for all who are left." The eschatological manna is mentioned in the same context.

17. Farrer, 292.

18. As in the earlier chapters, the quoted words in this section are from the Greek translation of the Hebrew Bible known as the Septuagint (LXX). However, unlike the previous chapter where several whole sentences from Deuteronomy were cited, here only key words, with the exception of a possible text from Exodus 16:15, are cited. Italics within Scripture passages are my own addition.

    Since the words are taken from the LXX of Exodus 16, scholars have missed these verbal cues from the passage after which the NT story is modeled. Consequently, most of the following observations are not found elsewhere in scholarly literature.

19. Borgen, 42. Also see pages 43, 54, 66, and 67.

20. On the other hand, one could argue that the words from Mark's "text" are repeated because they reflect the repetition of the same words in Exodus 16. Accordingly, "bread" is found seven times in Exodus 16, "eat" seven times, and "give" four times.

21. Taylor, 321; Donfried, 98.

22. Werner H. Kelber, *The Kingdom in Mark* (Philadelphia: Fortress, 1974), 55.

23. John Dominic Crossan, "The Seed Parables of Jesus," *JBL* 92 (1973): 256–57.

24. Note what Kelber says concerning the importance of this movement by boat: "it is the main purpose of the elaborate *mise en scène* 6:31–33 to locate it at a place near the *western* bank of the lake" (55). The impor-

tance of this geographical point will be discussed in the last section of this chapter. It is interesting that critical scholarship has established the sabbath and the manna as the two main emphases in Exodus 16. These ideas are found after the word "place," as pointed out above. See Malina, 16ff.

25. Taylor, 318.

26. Kelber, 56. Kelber assigns to the tradition only the reference to Jesus' compassion.

27. Malina, 86–89. The tradition that Moses was the shepherd of Israel can be dated to the first century A.D. See Pseudo-Philo, *LAB* 19:3, p. 327.

28. Mielziner, 143.

29. Bertil Gärtner, *John 6 and the Jewish Passover*, Coniectanea Neotestamentica XVII (Lund, Sweden: Gleerup, 1959), 16. See p. 16, n. 1, for references to this midrash.

30. II Baruch 29:8, *The Old Testament Pseudepigrapha*, 1:631. For a discussion concerning the date, see 617.

31. Malina, 101. Note how the Mekilta further agrees with Revelation 2:17 and Second Baruch: "R. Eleazar Hisma says: "You will not find it in this world but you will find it in the world to come." See *Mekilta de-Rabbi Ishmael*, Exod. 16:25, 2:119.

32. Gärtner, 19. See also Wayne Meeks, *The Prophet-King: Moses Traditions and the Johannine Christology*, Suppl., Novum Test., vol. 14 (Leiden: Brill, 1967), 98.

33. Vermes, "He is the Bread," in *Post-Biblical Jewish Studies* (Leiden: Brill, 1975), 142f.

34. *The Old Testament Pseudepigrapha*, 2:329. Later rabbis ascribed these gifts to the "merits" of these three and further exalted the figure of Moses. See Vermes, "He is the Bread," 141ff.

35. Josephus, *Antiquities* 3:26, quoted from Vermes, "He is the Bread," 143.

36. Borgen, 61ff. Also see the discussion in Malina, 86ff. Perhaps the tradition that Moses was the shepherd of Israel is related to these traditions concerning Moses' role in the descent of the manna (see n. 27, above).

37. Meeks, 214. The phrase "prophet-king" is found on p. 99.

38. Brown, 249–50.

39. Brown, 245.

40. I. De La Potterie argues forcefully for this interpretation in "Le sens primitif de la multiplication des pains," *Jésus aux origines de la Christologie*, ed. Jacques Dupont (Louvain: Leuven U. Press, 1975), 325f. De La Potterie argues on the basis of the Jewish hopes of the period which were discussed in the previous section on Jewish tradition.

41. Meeks, 99.
42. Achtemeier, 208–209, and De La Potterie, 319f.
43. Achtemeier, 208.
44. Samuel Tobias Lachs, *A Rabbinic Commentary on the New Testament* (Hoboken: KTAV, 1987), 241. See also Duncan Derrett, "Leek-beds and Methodology," *Biblische Zeitschrift* 19 (1975): 101–103. The fact that both expressions—by companies and in groups (verse 40)—are characterized by repetition may be evidence of Markan redaction. See De La Potterie, 314, n. 40.
45. De La Potterie, 320.
46. Gärtner, 17f.
47. Meeks, 99. David Daube argues even more strongly than do Borgen and Malina (see n. 36, above) that Moses brought down the manna. He maintains that this tradition was suppressed when the Passover Haggadah was fixed. See his article "The Earliest Structure of the Gospels," *NTS* 5 (1958–59): 178, n. 2.
48. Bammel, 216.
49. De La Potterie, 314.
50. However, if Vermes is correct in his analysis of Targum Neophyti to Exodus 16:15, even this high Johannine Christology is dependent on the manna tradition about Moses. In the targum, Moses speaks of himself in the third person and says, "He is the bread which the Lord has given you to eat." Moses, who is associated with manna and Torah, identifies "himself . . . as the heavenly bread itself, a personification of the divine nourishment allotted by God to Israel." See Vermes, "He is the Bread," 144–45.
51. Kelber, 57 and 61. A good discussion of the overall eschatological outlook of Mark's Gospel is found in Kee, *Community of the New Age*.

Chapter 4

1. Fitzmyer, 792.
2. M. Sabbé, "La rédaction du récit de la transfiguration," *La Venue du Messie*, Recherches Bibliques, 6 (Louvain: 1962), 75. For the specific emphases in Second Peter's account see J. Neyrey, "The Apologetic Use of the Transfiguration in 2nd Peter 1:16–21," *CBQ* 42 (1980), 509. Second Peter seems to depend on Matthew's account of the words from heaven for the phrase "with whom I am well pleased." Luke alone uses the word "glory" which Second Peter emphasizes.

3. G. Sellin, "Das Leben des Gottessohnes," *Kairos: Zeitschrift für Religionswissenschaft und Theologie*, Neuefolge 25 (1983): 242. Also see B. D. Chilton, "The Transfiguration: Dominical Assurance and Apostolic Vision," *NTS* 27 (1980–81): 119.

4. Kee, "The Transfiguration in Mark," *Understanding the Sacred Text*, ed. J. Reumann (Valley Forge: Judson, 1972), 139. Sabbé (80ff.) repeatedly stresses "the original literary unity" of the story.

5. Robert H. Stein, "Is the Transfiguration (Mark 9:2–8) a Misplaced Resurrection-Account?" *JBL* 95 (1976): 91.

6. Victor Furnish, *II Corinthians*, Anchor Bible, 32A (Garden City, NY: Doubleday, 1984), 240f. See also J. Behm, "*metamorphoo*," *TWNT*, 4: 758f.

7. Kee, "The Transfiguration," 144.

8. C. Rowland, *The Open Heaven: A Study of Apocalyptic in Judaism and Early Christianity* (New York: Crossroad, 1982), 366f. and n. 40. The fact that the same Greek term is also used with resurrection appearances does not mean the transfiguration is a resurrection appearance, as Stein has shown (see n. 5, above).

9. Sabbé, 67.

10 Sabbé, 69; see also 70.

11 Kee, "The Transfiguration," 149.

12. Sabbé, 67; also, see 70. Kee himself identifies the transfiguration as an apocalyptic vision ("The Transfiguration," 149–50), and further argues that his list of common details shows that Mark 9:2–8 is dependent upon Daniel 10. This conclusion does not necessarily follow. The list may simply indicate characteristics of the form.

13. Sabbé, 85.

14. Kee, "The Transfiguration," 147.

15. Chilton, 122.

16. Sabbé, 66–68.

17. I Enoch 1:2–4, *The Old Testament Pseudepigrapha*, 1: 13.

18. The Fourth Book of Ezra 14:1–7, *The Old Testament Pseudepigrapha*, 1: 553. This apocalyptic work, originally written in Hebrew, was "published" in Palestine about A.D. 100. See also 520.

19. Rowland, 51f. Rowland classifies the book as an apocalypse, but others as a midrash.

20. Furnish, 214.

21. Kee, "The Transfiguration," 146.

22. J. Jeremias, "Moses," *TWNT*, 4: 858ff.

23. Fitzmyer, 793. But see Donald Juel, *Messianic Exegesis* (Philadelphia: Fortress, 1988), 18, 62, 77.
24. Kee, "The Transfiguration," 147. Kee's concise summary of the scholarship concerning booths is very helpful.
25. Rowland, 368, and esp. n. 47. Rowland posits Peter as the original recipient of the vision.
26. Vermes, *Jesus the Jew* (New York: Macmillan, 1973), 211. Also see James D. G. Dunn, *Christology in the Making* (Philadelphia: Westminster, 1980), 26–28. Dunn speaks of Jesus' *abba* prayer and his sense of *"eschatological uniqueness* in his relationship with God," as conveyed through such passages as Mark 12:6 and Luke 22:29f. (28).
27. Kee, *Community of the New Age*, 123.
28. Kee, "The Transfiguration," 144; and *Community of the New Age*, 123.
29. Fitzmyer comes to much the same conclusion: "he is, nevertheless, heaven's Son . . . to whom human beings must now listen for their relation to God's kingdom" (794).
30. J. Neyrey, "The Apologetic Use of the Transfiguration in 2nd Peter 1:16–21," *CBQ* 42 (1980): 519.
31. Hans Dieter Betz, *Essays on the Sermon on the Mount* (Philadelphia: Fortress, 1985), 151ff. Betz finds that Matthew redacted an early Jewish Christian source in composing his Sermon on the Mount.
32. Kee, *Community of the New Age*, 75. I have reproduced Kee's thought in the following paragraph. See also Kee, 76.

Chapter 5

1. See Betz, esp. chap. 1, and Juel, *Messianic Exegesis* (Philadelphia: Fortress, 1981).
2. D. Daube, *The Exodus Pattern in the Bible* (London: Faber and Faber, 1963), 11ff.
3. Gärtner, 17f.
4. Martin Hengel, *The Son of God* (London: SCM, 1976), 90. I am indebted to Hengel for the above insight, although he spoke of earliest Christianity rather than early Jewish Christianity.
5. Hengel, 7–15. See esp. chap. 6. Also see Vermes, *Jesus the Jew* (New York: Macmillan, 1973), chap. 8, and esp. 209ff.
6. W. D. Davies, 116f.
7. Hengel, 2.

Index of Subjects and Names

Abraham
    Isaac's obedience to, 115
    love for Isaac, 19
    midrash on, 71
    sacrifice of Isaac, 13–31, 46, 51, 94,
        97, 100, 110–111
Achtemeier, P. J., 60, 75–76
Acts, book of, 95, 112
analogy of expressions (*Gezera Shava*),
    27, 69
angels, 47
apocalyptic
    genre, 88, 91–93, 97, 100, 109
    Judaism, 85–87, 91, 93, 109
    traditions, 95
    vision, 86, 98, 100, 102, 112

Bammel, E., 56, 79
baptism of Jesus, 13–31, 55, 84, 115–117
    and binding of Isaac, 13–31, 51, 61,
        100, 106, 113, 115
    and deliverance at the sea, 108
    formulation of early Jewish Christians,
        10
    herald of time of deliverance, 51
    and transfiguration, 91, 96–97, 100
    and wilderness generation, 49
Belial, 39; *see also* Satan
Betz, H. D., 101, 105
binding of Isaac, *see* Isaac
Borgen, P., 73
Brown, R., 53, 74, 76
Bultmann, R., 13–14, 34, 44–45, 54–55

catechetical instruction
    feeding five thousand narrative, 76
    temptation narrative, 50
chiastic arrangement, 64
    final expression in, 64–65
Chilton, B., 84, 90
Christian scribes, 43–48
Christology
    baptism narrative, 26–31
    divine man, 85, 87, 100
    early Jewish Christian community,
        107, 110–111
    feeding narrative, 77–81
    Gospel of John, 115–116
    Messiah-King, 105, 115
    temptation narrative, 47–48
    term "Son," 114–116
    transfiguration narrative, 85, 99–103
    see also typology
Chronis, H. L., 27–28
context, use in Jewish exegetical practice,
    36
criticism, biblical
    baptismal narrative, 13–14
    feeding narrative, 53–61
    temptation narrative, 33–35
    transfiguration narrative, 83–87
    see also form criticism; redaction
        criticism; source criticism
Crossan, J. D., 64

dating, problems of
    and exegetical traditions, 8–9, 16

dating, problems of (*cont.*)
  and NT narratives, 9–10
  and targumic accounts, 28–30
Davies, W. D., 60
Dead Sea Scrolls
  community of, 11, 30, 38, 57, 108
  comparison with early Jewish
    Christian school, 8, 112–114
  Exodus/Sinai/Wilderness cycle in,
    114
  final deliverance in, 51
  imitation of Israel's wilderness
    organization, 57, 108
  prophet like Moses in, 93
  testing sons of light in, 46
  wilderness tradition in, 8, 11, 37–40,
    51
De La Potterie, I., 74–75
Deute-Vision, see vision
devil, *see* Satan
Dibelius, M., 55
divine man, 85, 87, 100
Dodd, C. H., 84
dove (in baptism narrative), 23–24
Dupont, J., 44–45
Dunn, J. D. G., 18

early Jewish Christianity
  apocalyptic mindset of, 95
  apologetic activity of, 114
  Christology of, 28, 79, 99–100, 110–
    111, 114–116
  definition of, 2
  eschatological view of, 99–103, 109,
    111–112
  formulating work of, 9, 24–26, 48, 74,
    78, 89, 106
  history of, 1–2
  school of, 112–114
  self-understanding of, 8, 78, 101–102,
    107, 111–114
  spirituality of, 102, 112
  theology of, 8, 13, 97, 106–107
  treatment of feeding narratives, 77–81
  treatment of transfiguration, 95–103
  understanding of Jesus as Son of God,
    48–51, 96–98, 106
  use of Hebrew Bible, 4, 7, 13

view of history, 5, 51, 72, 77–78, 100,
    109
Ebionites, 1–2, 110–111
Elijah
  eschatological figure, 93, 96, 98
  in transfiguration narratives, 86–90,
    93–94, 96, 98
Elisha, 60–61
Emmanuel, 116
epiphany
  in feeding narratives, 55–56
  in transfiguration narratives, 84–85
eschatology
  eschatological authority, 87, 93, 99,
    101–102, 109–111
  eschatological community, 74, 78,
    101–102, 111–112, 114
  eschatological glorification, 85, 87, 98,
    102–103, 108–110
  in manna tradition, 56, 72–73, 74–81,
    112–113
  in Sinai tradition, 91–94, 108–109,
    113
  in wilderness tradition, 38–39, 51, 79
eucharist, 5, 55–61, 68, 75–81, 112
exegetical traditions
  binding of Isaac, 15–16, 19, 21, 24, 29,
    97, 113
  dating, 8–9
  definition, 7
  manna tradition, 56, 72–74, 77
  Moses and Sinai tradition, 86–87, 91–
    94, 108, 113
  rebuke tradition, 40–45, 47–49, 106,
    113
  wilderness tradition, 7–8, 37–49
Exodus
  as pattern for future deliverance, 107–
    110
  see also typology
Exodus/Sinai/Wilderness cycle, 105–
    110, 114

Farrer, A. M., 59, 60–61
feast of booths, 94, 96
feeding of the five thousand, 53–81
  Christology of, 106, 110

critical treatments of, 6, 10–11, 53–61
eschatological meanings of, 56, 109,
    111–113
as Lord's Supper, 55–61, 112
self-understanding of Jewish
    Christians in, 111–112
feeding of the four thousand, 54–55, 58
final expression, 64–65
Fitzmyer, J., 35, 46, 56, 94, 96
form criticism, 5, 10, 20–22
    failures of, 5–6, 106
    treatment of baptism narrative, 20–22
    treatment of feeding narrative, 55–56,
        75
    treatment of temptation narrative, 33–
        35
    treatment of transfiguration narrative,
        84–85, 99
formulators of the story
    see also Christian scribes 7, 11, 75, 81,
        89, 95, 112–114
Funk, R., 38

Galilean community, 115
Galilean ministry of Jesus, 53–54, 74
Gärtner, B., 77, 109
genetic analysis, 6–8
    see also Gerhardsson
Gerhardsson, B., 6–8, 14–15, 35, 46, 49–
    53, 83, 106
Gezera Shava (analogy of expressions),
    27, 69
golden calf, 41, 44–45

Haggadah, 34, 72
Halacha, 34
Hayward, R., 29–30
hellenistic-Jewish milieu, 85
Hengel, M., 111, 115
history
    Jewish Christian view of, 77–78, 100,
        109
    question of, 10–11
    theological view of, 108–109, 111
    theology and history, 24
    typological view of, 5, 51, 72, 79, 100
Holy Spirit, see Spirit

inclusion, technique of, 62–63, 70
interpretive vision, see vision
Isaac
    beloved son, 12, 17–20, 51, 85, 96–97,
        100, 110–111
    binding of, 13–31, 46, 51, 61, 94, 106,
        109
    exegetical traditions, 15–16, 19–24,
        113
    obedience of, 115
Isaiah, Second, 108

Jeremias, J., 94
Jerusalem community, 1, 115
Jewish Christianity, see early Jewish
    Christianity
Jewish tradition
    dating, 5, 8–9, 16
    definition, 7
    use of citations, 36
    see also exegetical traditions
John, Gospel of
    apologetic use of Exodus motif, 114
    high Christology of, 115–116
    meaning of "Son of God," 116
    treatment of delayed second coming,
        112
    treatment of feeding narrative, 10–11,
        53–54, 56–57, 71–76, 78–81, 108,
        110
Josephus, 15, 20, 30, 73, 108, 114
Jubilees, 19, 25, 43–44, 92, 113
Juel, D., 105, 115

Keck, L. E., 10, 30
Kee, H. C., 57, 84–87, 93, 97–99, 102
Kelber, W., 80

Lachs, S., 76
Lentzen-Deis, F., 20–23, 25, 30
Longenecker, R., 2
Lord's Supper, see Eucharist
Luke, Gospel of
    treatment of delayed second coming,
        112
    treatment of feeding narrative, 56, 62–
        63, 67–69, 71

Luke, Gospel of (*cont.*)
  treatment of temptation narrative, 33–35
  treatment of transfiguration, 83, 91, 95

Maccabees, IV, 30
manna
  in feeding narratives, 56–62, 65–81 107, 112
  foreshadows Lord's Supper, 5
  grumbling over, 41, 45
  new life in Christ as, 117
  sign of new age, 56, 72, 74, 77–78, 87, 109, 111–112
  in temptation narrative, 4, 47
  tradition, 56, 72–81, 87
Mark, Gospel of
  earliest gospel, 10, 16
  eschatological outlook of, 103
  theology of the cross, 26–27
  treatment of baptism narrative, 13, 16, 106, 110
  treatment of feeding narrative, 53–81, 106, 113
  treatment of temptation narrative, 33
  treatment of transfiguration, 83–86, 103
Marmorstein, A., 24–25
Marshall, I. H., 18, 96
Mastema, 19, 46
  see also Satan
Matthew, Gospel of
  apologetic use of Exodus motif, 114
  Son of God in, 115–116
  treatment of feeding narrative, 53–54, 62–64, 67–69, 71
  treatment of temptation narrative, 33–34
  treatment of transfiguration, 83, 86, 91, 95
Mauser, U., 58
McNamara, M., 25
Meeks, W., 73, 78–79
Messiah
  in baptism narrative, 14
  in Josephus, 108
  linked with return of manna, 60, 72, 109
  Mark's identification of Jesus as, 102

Messiah-King Christology, 105, 115
messianic banquet, 81, 109
no relation to "Son of God," 19–20 49–50, 94, 96, 111
view of Jerusalem community, 115
method, questions of, 5–11, 14–15, 42–43
midrash
  Christian midrash, 8, 35, 113
  compilation, editing, and dating, 29
  interplay of words and scenes, 71
  NT dependence on, 9
  numerical coincidence in, 70
Moses, 13–14, 33, 36–41, 43–45, 47–48, 77–78
  and manna, 59–62, 66–68, 72–75 107, 112
  Mosaic age, 51, 106
  parallel with Jesus, 14, 47–48, 78–79 107–108
  prophet like Moses, 79–80, 91, 93, 96–97, 107–108
  prophet-king, 73–75, 79–80
  in transfiguration, 86–99

narrative, use of, 3–4, 77
  definition and use of term, 3
  interpretive vision as a narrative form, 26
  narrative criticism, 3
  see also story

parable, 4–5, 41
parallel
  final deliverance, 51, 108
  Jesus and Isaac, 13, 21–22, 28–29, 31 51, 97, 106, 110
  Jesus and Moses, 48–49, 74, 78
  temptations of Israel and Jesus, 8, 44, 46–51, 65, 108, 113
  as a theological method, 109
  wilderness and feeding narrative, 58–61, 75, 78
  see also typology
Passover, 72, 74, 76
Paul, Apostle
  enemy of Ebionites, 2
  equates manna and eucharist, 59, 78, 80

fulfillment view of history, 77–78, 108
Jesus as more than Moses, 98
literary activity as basis for dating
    narratives, 30
Paul and pre-Pauline views of term
    "Son," 94, 96
recipient of visions, 95
reference to Jewish Christians, 1
typological views of Jesus, 4–5
use of *metamorphoo*, 85
use of Sinai tradition, 83
use of wilderness generation, 50–51,
    80
Philo, 30, 73
pre-Gospel source, *see* source criticism
pre-Markan tradition, *see* source criticism
Pseudo-Philo, 30, 73
psychologizing, 13–14

Q, 10, 34–35
Quesnell, Q., 57
Qumran, *see* Dead Sea Scrolls

rebuke tradition, 40–45, 47–49, 106, 113
    in targums, 40–43
    in NT, 44–45, 47
redaction criticism, 54–55, 58, 84, 95
    Markan redaction, 55, 58, 60, 63–67,
        79, 84, 95
Revelation, book of, 102
Richardson, A., 14, 49

Sabbé, M., 86
Satan (devil), 3, 46–48
    breaking power of, 51, 109–111
    initiates temptation of Jesus, 3, 36, 46–
        48
    see also Belial; Mastema
Second Isaiah, 108
Second Peter, book of, 99
Sellin, G., 84
Septuagint (LXX, Greek OT), 35, 113
    of Genesis (22), 17–20
    of Exodus (16), 61–72
    of Exodus (24), 88–90
    of Exodus (34), 89
    of Deuteronomy (6 and 8), 36–37
    of Deuteronomy (34), 47–48
    of Daniel (10), 86

Shekinah, 22–25, 30
Shema, 50–51
Sinai, Mount
    exegetical traditions, 43, 86–87, 91–
        94, 108, 115
    in temptation narrative, 4, 36
    in transfiguration narrative, 73–103
    see also Exodus/Sinai/Wilderness
        cycle
son
    beloved Son, 13, 17–20, 28, 50–51, 85,
        87, 91, 94, 97, 100–101, 106, 110–
        111, 114–115
    Israel as, 49
    not a messianic title, 13–14, 18–20,
        27–28, 49–50, 94–96, 100, 115
    Son of God, 3, 22, 27, 35, 44–
        51, 88, 94–98, 100–101, 106, 110–
        111, 114–116
source criticism, 33–34
    pre-Gospel source of feeding
        narratives, 53–54, 57, 59
    pre-Gospel source of temptation
        narrative, 33–34
    pre-Gospel source of transfiguration
        narrative, 84, 91, 95
    pre-Markan tradition, 10, 53–54, 59–
        60, 70, 84, 91, 95
spies (from Paran), 41, 43
Spirit
    of God, 46
    Holy Spirit, 23–26, 85, 116
spiritualizing
    definition, 73
    in manna tradition, 73, 79, 107, 110
Stein, R., 84–85
story
    form of Jewish Christian theology, 3–
        4, 28, 33
    world of, 4–5, 7
    see also narrative
Succoth (feast of booths), 94, 96
symbolism
    in feeding narratives, 6, 55–56, 60, 70,
        74–77
    manna symbolism, 56, 60, 74–77

Talmud, 42

Talmud (*cont.*)
"Fathers according to Rabbi Nathan," 42, 43, 45
Tannaitic literature, 22, 25, 42
targum
  dating, 28–30
  definition, 18
  of Deuteronomy (1:1), 41, 106
  Fragmentary Targum (J II), 21, 26, 41, 43
  of Genesis (22), 20–26, 28–30, 106
  Neofiti (Tg N), 21, 41, 43
  NT dependence on, 9
  Onkelos, 41
  on Psalm (2:7), 18
  Pseudo-Jonathan (J I), 21, 41
  terms for God, 22–23
Taylor, V., 35, 54–63
temptation of Jesus, 33–51, 55
  as catechetical instruction, 50
  Christology of, 110
  as dramatic creation, 50
  inauguration of age of salvation, 51, 109
  manna tradition in, 4, 79
  in Matthew, 6
  as midrash, 8
  parallels with Moses, 114
  wilderness wanderings in, 4, 7, 14, 33
test of Abraham, 46
test of Israel, 45–50
theology
  of baptismal narrative, 28, 31
  of the cross in Mark, 26–27
  of feeding narrative, 77–81
  of history, 108, 111
  history and theology, 11, 24, 51
  in narrative form, 28, 33, 77, 111
  of temptation narrative, 47–51
  theological motifs of Jewish Christians, 8, 107–109
  of transfiguration, 99–103
  in typological forms, 77, 100, 109
  use of term, 2–3
transfiguration, 83–103
  Christology of, 108–110, 117
  dramatic creation of, 95
  parallel with Moses, 114

self-understanding of Jewish Christians, 112
unity of, 83–84, 95
see also eschatology, in Sinai tradition
typology
  definition, 4–5
  Exodus/Sinai/Wilderness, 105–110 114
  Isaac–Jesus, 28, 31, 97, 100, 106, 110
  manna–eucharist, 77–78
  Moses–Jesus, 77–80, 107
  OT–NT, 100, 106
  use in theology, 100, 109
  wilderness generation–early Jewish Christian community, 78–80, 100
  wilderness generation–Jesus, 107–108
  see also parallel

unique aspects of this study, 105–107
  examination of common vocabulary. 17–20, 36–37, 61–72, 87–91

Vermes, G., 9, 22, 29, 97, 111
vision
  apocalyptic vision, 86–87, 95, 99, 100 102
  in baptism narrative, 21–22
  interpretive vision (*Deute-Vision*), 21–22, 25–26
  in Jewish Christian community, 100, 112
  in Mark, 16
  transfiguration as, 85–87, 98
vocabulary, common
  between Genesis 22 and baptism, 17–20
  between Exodus 16 and the feeding, 61–72
  between Exodus 24 and 34 and the transfiguration, 87–91
  between Deuteronomy 6 and 8 and the temptation, 36–37
voice from heaven, 13–14, 17–23, 24, 29. 84, 87, 89, 114–115

wilderness
  in baptism narrative, 61
  in Dead Sea Scrolls, 8, 11, 37–40
  eschatological tradition, 37

Exodus/Sinai/Wilderness cycle, 105–110, 114
in feeding narratives, 56–59, 64–70, 74
generation, 42–51, 70, 78–80, 98, 107–108
grass in, 76

sins of Israel in, 7, 40–51, 96
in temptation narrative, 4, 6–7, 14, 36–51
wanderings, 7, 31, 47, 56, 87, 107
world of story, *see* story

Zion, Mount, 115

Index of References

Old Testament

Genesis
3:22 21
18 71
22 ... 13, 14–21, 23–26,
    28–29, 46, 94, 97,
    106, 110, 113
22:1 46
22:2 ... 2, 13, 17–18, 23
22:4 17
22:10 ...... 19, 21–22
22:11 17
22:12 .... 14, 17–18, 23
22:14 .... 17, 21
22:15 17
22:16 ...... 17–18, 23
28:12 21
35:9 86
35:13 86

Exodus
13:17 73
15:27 70
16 .... 4, 56, 58, 61–71,
    77, 106
16:1 69
16:3 40
16:4 .... 61, 67, 71
16:6 67
16:8 67–70
16:9 67
16:12 67–68
16:13 67
16:13–15 75
16:15 . 61, 64, 67, 69–71

16:16 71
16:17 66
16:22 66
16:23 65–66
16:29 .... 64–65, 68
16:30 64
16:31 64
16:32 65–66
16:35 67
17:1 .... 4, 69
17:2 44
17:7 46–47
18:21 .... 57, 68
19:16 92
24 ... 83, 86–87, 89–92,
    93, 95–96, 108
24:1 88
24:2 88
24:9 88
24:10 89
24:11 89
24:12 92
24:13 88–89
24:15–16 90
24:16 .... 87, 89
24:17 92
25 89
25:8 88
26 88
27 88
32 4
33:1 43
34:28 48
34:29–35 . 86–87, 89–91,
    93–96, 108

34:30 89–90
34:35 89

Leviticus
22:47 19
23:43 88

Numbers
11 .... 58–59, 61
11:9 67
11:22 59
11:31–32 67
13:3 43
13:26 43
14:22 42
27:17 .... 58, 67

Deuteronomy
1:1 ...... 37, 40–43, 49,
    106, 113
1:2 41
6:4ff 50
6:13 .... 6, 36, 47
6:14 .... 36, 47
6:16 ...... 6, 36, 46–47
8:1–5 46
8:2 .... 36, 46
8:3 ... 6, 36, 73, 79, 107
8:3–16 69
8:5 36
8:10 69
9:4 23
9:9 48
9:18 48
9:22 42

Deuteronomy (*cont.*)
9:23 43
18:15 .. 91, 93, 107, 114
18:16 91
30:20 43
31:20 43
31:27 43
34:1 47

Joshua
5:10–12 72

Judges
6:21 86
13:3 86
13:20 86

1 Kings
19 96

2 Kings
4:42–44 60–61

Psalms
2:7 ...... 14, 17–20, 93,
                            97
44:23 23

Proverbs
28:23 41

Isaiah
6:6–7 21
40:3 38
42:1 .... 17, 19–20

Ezekiel
34:5 67

Daniel
10 .... 86, 91
10:1 86
12:8 86

Zechariah
14:16 94

Malachi
3 93

4 93
4:5 93

New Testament
Matthew
1:23 116
4:1 .... 36, 46
4:1–11 33
4:2 .... 36, 46
4:3 .... 36, 46–47
4:4 36
4:7 36
4:8 47–48
4:10 36
4:11 46
7:21–23 101
12:43 39
14:15 64
14:17 60
17:1–8 83
17:2 91
17:9 86

Mark
1:9 17
1:9–11 18–19
1:10 21
1:11 .... 13, 17, 21, 27,
                    91, 110
1:12–13 33
6:30 64–66
6:30–33 .... 55, 64
6:30–34 ..... 54, 61, 79
6:31 .... 58, 62–65, 70
6:31–34 63
6:32 .... 58, 63–65
6:33 66–69
6:34 ..... 58, 63, 66–67,
                        79
6:35–44 ..... 54–55, 70
6:36 .... 62–63, 67
6:37 ... 62–63, 67, 69–
                        70
6:38 .... 63, 66–68
6:39 .... 63, 68, 76
6:40 .... 63, 68
6:41 .... 60, 62, 68
6:42 .... 62–63, 69

6:43 .... 63, 69
6:44 .... 62–63, 70
8:1–10 .... 54, 80
8:6 78
8:29 102
8:38 .... 99, 101
9:2 .... 88–89, 91
9:2–8 .... 83, 86, 90, 99,
                        102
9:3 83
9:4 ...... 86, 88–89, 93
9:5 .... 88–89, 94
9:6 90
9:7 ...... 84–85, 88, 93,
                        105
9:8 ...... 84–86, 88, 89
9:9–10 86
10:38 27
10:45 28
12:17 10
13 102
14:42 68
15:37–39 27
15:38 27

Luke
1:11 86
4:1–13 33
9:12–13 64
9:28–36 83
9:29 91

John
6 61
6:10 76
6:11 .... 75, 78
6:12 71
6:14 .... 78, 93, 108
6:14–15 .. 11, 56, 72–74,
                    79, 110
6:15 .... 76, 79
6:30–34 79
6:31 62–63
6:31–58 .. 56, 62, 71, 79
6:32 .... 73, 78
6:49 80
6:50 80
6:51 80
6:51–58 75

6:54 .... 64, 75
6:56 .... 64, 75
6:58 62
9:5 80

Acts
7:39–41 44
10:7 86
10:16 86
11:15ff 102

1 Corinthians
10:1–4 .... 58, 78
10:1–11 51
10:1–13 108
10:2–4 4
10:11 .... 51, 77, 80

2 Corinthians
3:7–14 98
3:7–18 108
3:18 .... 85, 92

1 Thessalonians
2:14 .... 1, 102

Hebrews
3:1–7 98

2 Peter
1:16–18 83

Revelation
2:17 72
4:5 92
7:13–14 85
11:19 86
12:1–3 86

Extrabiblical Literature

Apocrypha and Pseudepigrapha
II Baruch
  29:8   72
I Enoch
  1:2–4 91–92
  10:4 39
IV Ezra
  14:1–7 92
Jubilees
  17:18 46
Testaments of the Twelve Patriarchs
Testament of Levi
  18:6–7 26

Dead Sea Scrolls
Community Rule (1 QS)
  1:16–18 39
  3:22–25 39
  8:4 39
  8:13–15 38
Damascus Document
        41, 43–44, 113

Rabbinic Literature
Mekilta
  on Genesis 22 17
  on Exodus 13:17 .. 73
Midrash Rabbah
  on Genesis 18 71
  on Deuteronomy . 45
  on Deuteronomy
  1:2 41
  on Deuteronomy
  9:4 23
  on Song of Songs . 23
Mishna
  Pirqe Aboth 42
Sifrei
  on Deuteronomy
  1:1 .... 37, 40